Indochina Monographs

The South Vietnamese Society

Maj. Gen. Nguyen Duy Hinh and
Brig. Gen. Tran Dinh Tho

U. S. ARMY CENTER OF MILITARY HISTORY

WASHINGTON, D. C.

Library of Congress Cataloging in Publication Data

Hinh, Nguyen Duy.
 The South Vietnamese society.

 1. Vietnam--Social conditions. I. Tho, Tran Dinh,
joint author. II. Title. III. Series.
HN700.5.A8H55   309.1'597   79-17694

This book is not copyrighted and may be reproduced in
whole or in part without consulting the publisher

Reprinted 1984

CMH PUB 92-18

Indochina Monographs

This is one of a series originally published in limited quantity in 1980 by the U.S. Army Center of Military History. The continuous demand for these monographs has prompted reprinting. They were written by officers who held responsible positions in the Cambodian, Laotian, and South Vietnamese armed forces during the war in Indochina. The General Research Corporation provided writing facilities and other necessary support under an Army contract with the Center of Military History. The monographs were not edited or altered and reflect the views of their authors—not necessarily those of the U.S. Army or the Department of Defense. The authors were not attempting to write definitive accounts but to set down how they saw the war in Southeast Asia.

These works should provide useful source materials for serious historians pending publication of the more definitive series, the U.S. Army in Vietnam.

DOUGLAS KINNARD
Brigadier General, USA (Ret)
Chief of Military History

INDOCHINA MONOGRAPHS

TITLES IN THE SERIES
(title--author/s--LC Catalog Card)

The Cambodian Incursion--Brig. Gen. Tran Dinh Tho--79-21722 — CMH PUB 92-4

The Easter Offensive of 1972--Lt. Gen. Ngo Quang Truong--79-20551 — CMH PUB 92-13

The General Offensives of 1968-69--Col. Hoang Ngoc Lung--80-607931 — CMH PUB 92-6

Intelligence--Col. Hoang Ngoc Lung--81-10844/AACR2 — CMH PUB 92-14

The Khmer Republic at War and the Final Collapse--Lt. Gen. Sak Sutsakhan--79-607776 — CMH PUB 92-5

Lam Son 719--Maj. Gen. Nguyen Duy Hinh--79-607101 — CMH PUB 92-2

Leadership--General Cao Van Vien--80-607941 — CMH PUB 92-12

Pacification--Brig. Gen. Tran Dinh Tho--79-607913 — CMH PUB 92-11

RLG Military Operations and Activities in the Laotian Panhandle--Brig. Gen. Soutchay Vongsavanh--81-10934/AACR2 — CMH PUB 92-19

The RVNAF--Lt. Gen. Dong Van Khuyen--79-607963 — CMH PUB 92-7

RVNAF and U.S. Operational Cooperation and Coordination--Lt. Gen. Ngo Quang Truong--79-607170 — CMH PUB 92-16

RVNAF Logistics--Lt. Gen. Dong Van Khuyen--80-607117 — CMH PUB 92-17

Reflections on the Vietnam War--General Cao Van Vien and Lt. Gen. Dong Van Khuyen--79-607979 — CMH PUB 92-8

The Royal Lao Army and U.S. Army Advice and Support--Maj. Gen. Oudone Sananikone--79-607054 — CMH PUB 92-10

The South Vietnamese Society--Maj. Gen. Nguyen Duy Hinh and Brig. Gen. Tran Dinh Tho--79-17694 — CMH PUB 92-18

Strategy and Tactics--Col. Hoang Ngoc Lung--79-607102 — CMH PUB 92-15

Territorial Forces--Lt. Gen. Ngo Quang Truong--80-15131 — CMH PUB 92-9

The U.S. Adviser--General Cao Van Vien, Lt. Gen. Ngo Quang Truong, Lt. Gen. Dong Van Khuyen, Maj. Gen. Nguyen Duy Hinh, Brig. Gen. Tran Dinh Tho, Col. Hoang Ngoc Lung, and Lt. Col. Chu Xuan Vien--80-607108 — CMH PUB 92-1

Vietnamization and the Cease-Fire--Maj. Gen. Nguyen Duy Hinh--79-607982 — CMH PUB 92-3

The Final Collapse--General Cao Van Vien--81-607989 — CMH PUB 90-26

Preface

During the Vietnam conflict, the long and destructive war, Communist subversion, an unstable economy, several changes in government and the extended presence of Free World Military Forces combined to accentuate the basic weaknesses of South Vietnamese society: divisiveness and infighting.

To evaluate the effect that South Vietnamese society had on the conduct of the war, this monograph seeks to present the Vietnamese point of view on the joint U.S.-RVN efforts to build a strong and viable South Vietnam, the impact of U.S. aid and the American presence on the South Vietnamese society, the most significant social problems that South Vietnam faced during and as a result of the war, and finally the viability of the U.S.-supported regime and its leadership.

To provide this in-depth analysis we, the authors, have drawn primarily on our own experience as major witnesses of South Vietnam's politico-social tragedy and participants in the war effort. Constructed from the combined vantage points of our positions, one in the field and exposed to the rural scene and the other in the very heart of the urban mainstream, this work thoroughly reflects the insider's viewpoint and internate knowledge of South Vietnamese political and social life.

In the preparation of this monograph, we have interviewed several prominent South Vietnamese political and social leaders presently in the United States. Because of their insistence on anonimity, we think it proper to acknowledge their goodwill through a collective, impersonal expression of thanks. Additionally, we owe a special debt of gratitude to General Cao Van Vien, Chief of the Joint General Staff, JGS, Lieutetenant General Dong Van Khuyen, Chief of Staff, JGS, Lieutenant General Ngo Quang Truong, Commanding General, I Corps and MR-1, and Colonel Hoang Ngoc Lung, Assistant Chief of Staff J-2, JGS for their valuable guidance, perceptive remarks, and constructive suggestions.

Finally, I am particularly indebted to Lieutenant Colonel Chu Xuan Vien and Ms. Pham Thi Bong. Lt. Colonel Vien, the last Army Attache serving at the Vietnamese Embassy in Washington, D.C., has done a highly professional job of translating and editing that helps impart unity and cohesiveness to the manuscript. Ms. Bong, a former Captain in the Republic of Vietnam Armed Forces and also a former member of the Vietnamese Embassy staff, spent long hours typing, editing and in the administrative preparation of this monograph in final form.

McLean, Virginia
15 December 1978

Nguyen Duy Hinh
Major General, ARVN

Tran Dinh Tho
Brigadier General, ARVN

Contents

Chapter	Page
I. THE VIETNAMESE HERITAGE	1

Ancient Vietnamese Society and the Chinese Influence . . 1
The Vietnamese Spirit of Struggle in Ancient Times . . . 5
Vietnamese Society Under French Rule 7
*The Birth of Political Parties and The Resistance
   Movement* 9
A Society in Transition 13
Contact With Communism 15

II. THE CONSOLIDATION OF SOUTH VIETNAM 20

The Preliminary Conditions 20
Building Strength and A National Cause 28
Motivation of the People 43

III. AMERICAN INFLUENCE ON SOUTH VIETNAMESE SOCIETY 55

Significant Contrasts 55
Major Objectives and their Impact 58
Social Impact of the American Presence 65

IV. SOCIAL PROBLEMS 72

Discrimination and Factionalism 72
The Struggle of Political and Religious Groups 82
The Problem of Ethnic Minorities 96
The Impact of Communist Insurgency and Protracted War . 103

V. THE REGIME AND LEADERSHIP 122

South Vietnam and Democracy 122
Democracy and the Leadership of President Ngo Dinh Diem 128
Democracy and Leadership since November 1963 140

VI. OBSERVATIONS AND CONCLUSIONS 154

GLOSSARY 175

CHAPTER I

The Vietnamese Heritage

Ancient Vietnamese Society and the Chinese Influence

Vietnamese have always prided themselves as a people with four thousand years of civilization, two thousand of which is steeped in legends and the remaining enlightened by recorded history. Chinese historians wrote profusely about the Vietnamese people. One of their works, *Viet Tuyen Thu* (A Treatise on the Viets), described our people in these words: "The Viets are disdainful, belligerent, astute in military matters, and not afraid to die. They live in the mountains yet move about on water, using boats as vehicles and oars as horses. When they come, it is like a gentle breeze; when they go, it is hard to catch up with them."[1]

Chinese emperors of every dynasty had always wanted to assimilate the Vietnamese by subjugation and domination. The first period of Chinese rule extended for more than ten centuries, from 111 B.C. to A.D. 968, the year the Vietnamese regained their sovereignty. During this long period, which was highlighted by five uprisings of Vietnamese patriots, what surprised historians the most was not the deep Chinese influence on the Vietnamese but their ability to resist complete sinicization.

It was not that China had no serious design to assimilate the Viets. The fact was that after the first uprising had been put down in A.D. 40-43, the Chinese compelled Vietnamese to wear their clothes

---

[1] This book was written during the Han Dynasty, after their conquest of Vietnam that lasted from circa 100 B.C. to circa A.D. 102.

and hair in the Chinese-style, live the Chinese way of life, and pattern their village administration after the Chinese model. Despite this, the Vietnamese retained their identity and certain cultural traits of their own. These traits were found to be more accentuated in the masses than among the affluent bourgeoisie.

During the initial period of Chinese domination, the Vietnamese were still in a semi-civilized state. The Chinese brought their culture, philosophy, and literature into Vietnam not so much to "civilize" the Vietnamese as to facilitate and perpetuate their rule. This process of acculturation continued to expand as many generations of lettered and prominent Chinese subsequently took refuge in Vietnam as a result of civil strife and disturbances in their homeland.

The most profound Chinese influence on traditional Vietnamese society was perhaps Confucianism. The practice of Confucianism, which was founded by Confucius 500 years before the birth of Christ and later propagated by his nephew Mencius, was known as the Confucian-Mencian Way. Through the ages, Confucian-Mencian philosophy so thoroughly permeated Vietnamese politics, ethics, sociology, and even economics that it could be said to be the Vietnamese nation's religion from its birth to the beginning of French rule in 1883. Confucius's teachings were founded on the concept of natural law, which, in practical terms, translated into social order and social rules. Confucianism conceived of a nation as being one extended family in which the emperor was the father and the subjects his children. The personal morality of the ruler was of utmost importance since it exerted an encompassing influence on the people. Confucius said, "The ruler is like the wind and the commoners the grass blades. When the wind blows, the grass blades have to bend under it."

In his study of Confucianism, Pham Quynh, a Vietnamese scholar in the early 30's asserted: "Our society has two great classes, the common people who are rural peasants and the educated or (Confucianist) scholars. The commoners, always submissive and unenvious, look upon the scholars as teachers and guides. The scholars accept this responsibility obligingly and without arrogance; they consider themselves the missionaries of the Confucian-Mencian Way."[2]

The traditional social hierarchy depicted by Pham Quynh survived through generations and remained immutable until recent times. It included, in descending order, the scholars, the farmers, the craftsmen, and the merchants. Popular sentiment, however, did not always regard this established order as absolute. The supremacy of scholars, who usually shunned economic productivity, was often ridiculed by the more pragmatic common people. A popular saying in fact commented sarcastically, "They tell us that scholars come first and farmers second; all right. But when rice runs out and one is running around looking for it, then who should come first but the farmers?" This irreverent attitude toward scholars reflected the lesser extent of influence Confucianism exerted on the populace. The impact of Buddhism and Taoism, both also introduced by the Chinese, was perhaps much greater among them.

Buddhism came to Vietnam at the end of the second century B.C. and evolved through three periods, the first of which, the period of propagation, lasted until the sixth century. Buddhist philosophy observes that human beings are continually beset by sufferings from one life to the next. The sufferings that one endures in this life are the result of his doings in a previous life and actions in this life are the cause for sufferings in the next. The real cause of sufferings is man's greed; to eliminate sufferings, therefore, one must eliminate greed. From the seventh to the fourteenth century, Buddhism gained ascendency almost as a national religion in Vietnam. It was during this period that Vietnamese emperors adopted Chinese characters as the national script. Since Chinese Buddhist monks were also great literary scholars, they assumed the teaching of Chinese characters. The influence of Buddhism reached its apogee under the Ly and Tran

---

[2]<u>Nam Phong Tap Chi</u>, No. 172; Hanoi, May 1932.

dynasties whose emperors led a monastic life after abdicating from their thrones. The fifteenth century then saw the decline of Buddhism which increasingly came under attack by Confucianists. Buddhist monks gradually lost their scholarship and their grip on the true Buddhist creed; they eventually strayed into heresy, ritualism, and supertitious practices. Despite this, Buddhism remained a major religion in Vietnam with an estimated 80 percent of the population claiming to be adherents.

Aside from Buddhism, Vietnamese were also influenced by Taoism although to a lesser degree. Taoism was founded by a Chinese named Lao-Tzu at about the same time as Confucianism. Just as Mencius did for Confucianism, Chuang-Tzu, a disciple, continued to spread the Taoist philosophy and tradition after his master's death. Introduced in Vietnam under Chinese domination, Taoism had a broad following. However, because of the abstruseness of its ontology, perhaps very few understood it. The essence of Taoism lies in quietism and passivism, which implies that one must absolutely give up all concern and desire and ignore the bodily self in order to achieve spiritual purity and tranquility, a state of the mind devoid of all wishes and actions. Chuang-Tzu compared life to a dream. He told of a dream in which he was transformed into a butterfly; awake, he wondered whether he was a butterfly dreaming of becoming a man. Distorted interpretations of Taoism eventually degraded this philosophy into a popular creed characterized by superstition, magic, and sorcery and widely practiced by the Vietnamese common populace. Among the educated, the impact of Taoism was more philosophical. In general, it created a certain abhorrence of wealth and fame and the quest for an easy life and total freedom.

In short, the combined philosophies of Buddhism, Confucianism, and Taoism exerted a rather unique influence on traditional Vietnamese society: a steadfast adherence to fatalism or the belief that everything was predestined or preordained by mysterious causes. This was a trait that seemed to affect the drive for action among Vietnamese whether as individuals or as a community. In their everyday lives, Vietnamese cleaved to the sages' teachings, especially the Confucianist code of ethics, and tended to act in accordance with precepts embodied in old legends and stories. This dominant Chinese influence began to wane only upon contact with Western civilization during the French rule. However, in several aspects, it still lingers among the populace until today.

The Vietnamese Spirit of Struggle in Ancient Times

The permeating influence of Chinese civilization on Vietnam was never able to destroy the Vietnamese people's will to survive as a sovereign, independent nation and to expand that nation. This indomitable spirit manifested itself through the three main stresses of Vietnamese history: Resisting the North, Chastising the South, and Expanding Southward.

Resistance to the North was mainly directed against Chinese domination and aggression. Although during the thousand years of Chinese rule the Vietnamese had won back only three brief years of independence -- from 40 to 43 A.D. -- their insurrection was highlighted by the fact that it was led by two heroines, the Trung Sisters. At the command of an ill-trained, ill-equipped army of 60,000 men, the Trung Sisters succeeded in throwing out the Chinese administrators and troops of the Eastern Han Dynasty by the sheer force of their patriotism. The return of the Chinese army under Ma Yuan eventually forced the Trung Sisters to drown themselves in the Hat River, but even in defeat, this valorous act demonstrated the invincible Vietnamese spirit. "Rather dead than living in shame" had become the predominant trait of national survival ever since.

The history of Vietnamese resistance to foreign aggression includes other illustrious exploits such as Tran Hung Dao's routing of the invincible Mongols in the thirteenth century and the conquest of southern China in the early eighteenth century by Emperor Quang Trung whose forces occupied the city of Ung Chau under the Sung dynasty (1706) and destroyed all roads and bridges before they withdrew to pre-empt a Chinese invasion.

Besides resounding feats against foreign aggression, the Vietnamese also distinguished themselves by actions designed to punish belligerent peoples to the South and colonize their territories in the process. These actions were dictated by the need to remove a serious threat posed by Champa and Chenla (Cambodia) whose armies had repeatedly invaded since the second century A.D. (102). Then, at the turn of the 11th century (in the year 1044), the Vietnamese expansion southward began in earnest. By outright annexation, military conquests, or diplomatic maneuvers, this colonizing process did not end until the 18th century.

Two significant developments emerged during this southward movement. As national territory extended southward, the spirit of regionalism was born. It came as a result of difficulties in interregional communication, years of warfare or crop failure, insurgencies in many localities, and the weakening of royal authority with the concomitant strengthening of recalcitrant local authorities. This division of the country into regions each with its autonomous power eventually led to a feudal system with twelve warlords in the tenth century.

The second development was the establishment of villages. As the basic administrative unit, the Vietnamese village was autonomous and self-sufficient. The imperial court never dealt directly with villagers. It enforced laws, levied taxes, and impressed citizens into military service or work gangs through the intermediary of the village's council of notables who were elected by virtue of their titles, education, age, or wealth. This autonomous spirit led to each village having a separate charter which allowed the villagers to manage their own affairs and govern by themselves. Traditionally, therefore, Vietnamese liked to live in small communities. Their attachment and loyalties went first and foremost to their home villages.

Despite their isolation and limitations, villages constituted a true base from which southern expansion was launched. Rapid population growth and the inability of villages to expand beyond the confines of their bamboo hedges impelled villagers, especially young men and women without possessions, to pioneer and work adjacent lands and set up new villages with the assistance of old communities. Once the process was completed, the pioneering villagers reported to the emperor, who conferred a name to the new village, and upon their recommendation, decreed a titular god for the new community.

In general, from the time the nation was founded until the advent of French rule in the 19th century, the Vietnamese people had exhibited two remarkable traits: a disposition for endurance, patience, conservatism, and fatalism, which was instilled by Chinese doctrines; and a spirit of survival, independence, and expansion which manifested itself in times of national distress. Under French domination, these traits gradually underwent changes in order to adjust to the new circumstances. Accelerated by new developments in world currents, these changes gained strong momentum during the second half of the 19th century.

Vietnamese Society Under French Rule

Ancient Vietnamese society first came into contact with Europeans during the 16th century in the persons of Christian missionaries. Initially, these missionaries came and went, but in the 17th century they came to stay.

Because of policy differences between the Trinh lords in the North and the Nguyen emperor in the South, missionaries were eventually forbidden to preach their religion and the converts severely punished. Still, the missionaries kept coming surreptitiously and the number of converts kept growing. Under the reign of Emperor Tu Duc, who suspected the missionaries of having political motives, the Vietnamese royal court ordered their persecution, giving France's Emperor Napoleon III an excuse to invade Vietnam in 1857. Eventually this led to French occupation of Vietnam and the establishment of French rule in 1883.

At the time of the first French attack, Vietnam already encompassed all of its present-day territory. The Nguyen dynasty divided the country into three regions, the South, the Center, and the North and placed a royal governor at the head of each region to insure a unified administration.

When the French took over, they maintained the same territorial division, apparently not for the same purposes, but gave each region a different administrative status in accordance with their objective of "divide and rule." The South (Cochinchina) became a colony directly governed by the French while the Center (Annam) and the North (Tonkin) were French "protectorates." The Vietnamese emperor was given some token authority over Annam but real power remained in the hands of the French Resident General at the head of each region.

In a move to further degrade the authority of the imperial court, which was executed through the system of mandarins, the French eliminated the mandarinate by replacing it with a French-trained civil service. Beginning in 1903, a prerequisite for a mandarin in Tonkin and Annam was the ability to speak French; then came the abolition of competitive examinations held by the court for the purpose of selecting mandarins. These old-style examinations in Chinese classics were discontinued in Tonkin in 1915 and in Annam in 1918. To train middle-echelon bureaucrats and professionals, the University of Hanoi was founded in 1918. The educational system set up then by the French sought primarily to train low-level civil servants to fill minor positions in the administration, those that required no French citizenship. There was no effort on the part of French authorities during that period to change or reorganize village government, perhaps because they saw no need for such a move or because the existing system suited their policy of ruling by division.

There was the theory that the French reorganization of government at high levels and the absence of such an effort at the local level had been instrumental in fomenting resistance against colonial rule by the mandarin class. This resistance, which manifested through various Can Vuong (Restoration) movements led by such patriots as Emperor Ham Nghi, De Tham, and Phan Dinh Phung existed presumably because the mandarins' interests were being threatened. However rationalistic it might sound, this theory could not hold true because in the Vietnamese context of that time such insurrections could only be led by men of prestige.

In their effort to create a new upper class to replace the old mandarinate, the French had greater success in Cochinchina than in Tonkin or Annam. A new land annexed to Vietnam barely a century before French occupation, Cochinchina was pioneer country. The local settlers, under the influence of the new environment with its immense fertile plains and productive rivers, had simpler and more open minds. They were especially less bound to tradition and the restrictive influence of Confucianism than the conservative people of Tonkin and Annam. Cochinchina also came into contact with the French much earlier than the other two regions, and the French had succeeded in forging some degree of harmony with the local people. Early exposure to French culture enabled more Southerners to speak French and learn French ways; it also made their naturalization process much easier. A new class, therefore, emerged in Cochinchina which was made up of people in the French employ or having business relations with the French and large landowners. Benefiting from the French land development program during 1880-1939, these landowners eventually became the first indigenous bourgeois-capitalists of the whole country. With their favored treatment of this new rising class and their effort to win friends among Southerners by favoritist policies, the French managed to reinforce the spirit of regionalism that had been latent among Vietnamese.

In 1930, the French began to focus their attention on village government with an attempt to reduce village autonomy and the power of the council of notables and exert closer control over the rural peasantry. They instituted civil status records to include birth, death, and marriage so as to gain essential information for taxation purposes. They imposed strict control on matters of village finance and tax records and enacted laws to govern the council of notables and village charters. No longer was the village to enjoy the freedom of former times.

The changes in traditional Vietnamese society came about partially as a result of the French influence. While some of these changes were part of a systematic design, others, more important, came naturally from contacts with Western civilization and ideologies. It was this initiation to the Western world that spawned indigenous political parties and their tenacious struggle agianst French rule. These included both Vietnamese nationalist parties and the Indochinese Communist Party (ICP).

The Birth of Political Parties and The Resistance Movement

Familiarity with the French language and culture brought about beneficial results for the Vietnamese people. Through this language, Vietnamese had a chance to learn about new currents of thought and political doctrines unknown in traditional Vietnam such as individualism, democracy, and Marxism. Another benefit was the ability to think and reason independently on the part of the educated. In former times, the study of Chinese classics required a great deal of memorization since all Chinese characters have different shapes. And since education consisted primarily of rote learning, many old-time scholars lacked the ability to think and reason. This shortcoming was remedied by the logical approach of Western education. Western ideologies, therefore, gained in value and finally conquered an increasing number of classical scholars especially after the eye-opening Japanese-Russian War of 1904. Bigger and modernly equipped Russian ships, they had seen for themselves, were battered by the Japanese Navy and forced to take refuge in a Vietnamese port for repair. This was a shining example, not lost on Vietnamese intellectuals, of the kind of progress that a weak Oriental people with essentially the same civilization as the Vietnamese had been able to achieve by its early awakening and modernization efforts. The lesson learned by our intellectuals was that the mastery of Western technology and doctrines could well enable a small nation to defeat a Western power.

A movement for off-shore training gained popularity almost overnight with Phan Boi Chau and Prince Cuong De in the vanguard. Both went to Japan in 1906 and founded in exile the Duy Tan (Modernization) movement with the purpose of liberating the country from French rule, restoring the monarchy, and modernizing Vietnam after the Japanese model. Expelled by the Japanese who yielded to French pressure, Phan Boi Chau went to Thailand then China. By 1911, he had managed to forge a relationship with some leaders of the Kuomintang and founded the Viet Nam Quang Phuc Hoi (Vietnam Restoration Party) whose objective was to eliminate French rule and transform Vietnam into a republic like China.

Quang Phuc Hoi secretly conducted its operations in the country. Its undertakings included the assassination of collaborators loyal to the French and the 1916 unsuccessful armed attempt to free revolutionaries from French jails in Saigon. In 1925, betrayed by Nguyen Ai Quoc (Ho Chi Minh), Phan Boi Chau was arrested by the French; he spent the rest of his life in banishment.

After the Quang Phuc Hoi, the Viet Nam Quoc Dan Dang (Vietnam Kuomintang or Nationalist Party) came into being in 1927; its membership was overwhelmingly composed of the educated and people working for the French. Nguyen Thai Hoc was the leader of the Vietnam Nationalist Party (VNQDD). In February 1930, the VNQDD planned to launch an armed rebellion by Vietnamese soldiers serving in French forces who were party members to coincide with a popular uprising. A last-minute change in plans was not disseminated in time to all elements concerned and resulted in the premature revolt by two Vietnamese rifle companies stationed in Yen Bai. The unsuccessful coup at Yen Bai led to the French bombing of Co An Village, Hai Duong Province, where the VNQDD maintained its headquarters and to the capture and execution of Nguyen Thai Hoc and 13 of his comrades. In 1932 after the French had arrested 74 more party members, the rest of the VNQDD fled to Yunnan. Subsequently, although its name and fame continued, the VNQDD virtually ceased all of its activities inside Vietnam

Another party, the Dai Viet Quoc Dan Dang (Greater Vietnam Nationalist Party) better known as the Dai Viet, was founded in 1940. Most of its members were graduates of the Hanoi University. The party's creation came in the wake of France's occupation by the Nazis and after French authorities in Indochina had been forced to let the Japanese set up military installations there. Despite a formal agreement concluded between the French Governor General and the Japanese, fighting broke out between French and Japanese troops in Lang Son as soon as the latter moved in from southern China. During the Lang Son firefight, the Japanese allied themselves with members of the Vietnam Phuc Quoc Hoi, giving them weapons to fight against the French. However, once their objective had been accomplished through negotiations, the Japanese immediately abandoned the Phuc Quoc Hoi which was soon crushed by the French. The remainder of the party fled underground to reemerge only in March 1945 when the Japanese overthrew the French in Indochina.

While the VNQDD and Dai Viet were active in the North, Cochinchina witnessed the emergence of the Cao Dai and the Hoa Hao, two anti-French organizations which were at once religious and political.

The Cao Dai was founded in 1926. It was a creed which synthesized elements of Buddhism, Taoism, Confucianism, and Christianity. Its philosophy was based on the belief that every religion had its strong points and that the best religion was the one which combined the essence of all religions. Tay Ninh was the Holy See of the Cao Dai where lived the heaviest concentration of followers. Four years after its founding, to gain support in its opposition to the French, the Cao Dai proclaimed a policy of friendship towards the Japanese. This policy became pronounced under the leadership of Pope Pham Cong Tac. Realizing the potential threat of this religion, the French prohibited its propagation in Tonkin and Annam. In 1940, the French arrested Pope Pham Cong Tac and exiled him to Madagascar.

The Hoa Hao religious sect was born seven years after the Cao Dai. It gained ground mostly in the Western provinces of the Mekong Delta. The Hoa Hao creed was primarily Buddhist-oriented, but it also emphasized the cult of ancestors and the worship of national heroes. It viewed true devotion as stemming from the heart, not from formal rites. Therefore the Hoa Hao conducted worship services privately at home instead of at a pagoda. In its religious practice, each Hoa Hao family maintained an open-air altar in Buddha's honor, on which there were no offerings other than a single incense stick and a bowl of water. This simplicity of rites won over a large number of believers. In addition, the Hoa Hao founding father, Huynh Phu So, earned the admiration and trust of his followers through his ability to cure diseases with herbs and acupuncture. Like the Cao Dai, the Hoa Hao also advocated a policy of friendship with the Japanese in its efforts to resist the French. In 1940, Huynh Phu So was arrested by the French and jailed in Cai Be, My Tho Province. This only increased the veneration of his believers, and the number of Hoa Hao converts was growing day by day. Later, the French confined him to the Cho Quan mental institution where doctors were convinced of his perfect sanity. After his release, he continued to enjoy Japanese protection and secretly received Japanese weapons to equip his army.

The emergence of nationalist movements in Tonkin and Annam and of politically-motivated religious sects in Cochinchina together with the Communist front organization, the Viet Nam Doc Lap Dong Minh Hoi (League for Vietnam Independence) or Viet Minh, highlighted the Vietnamese spirit of resistance against foreign domination which had existed since ancient times. However, a great difference separated the Nationalists from the Communists; while the Communists always seemed united in their action, nationalist groups struggled separately without regard to common interests or a desire to coalesce into a unified national front.

This fact showed that traditionalism or conservatism coupled with the impact of French policies had debilitated the ranks of Vietnamese nationalists who seemed unable to rise above divisiveness and mutual suspicion. The major weakness of every nationalist group derived from the delusion that it alone was the champion of the national cause.

A Society in Transition

During her domination of Vietnam, France was involved in two world wars. World War I had compelled France to obtain resources from her colonies to satisfy the requirements of the war in Europe. In terms of human resources, France had impressed a total of 43,000 troops and 49,000 workers from Vietnam to serve in the French Army. To help finance the war effort, the French government also obtained funds from Vietnam by issuing treasury bonds under a program attractively called "the Vietnamese dragon spits money to help defeat Germany."

To exploit indigenous resources, the French operated rubber plantations in the South and coal mines in the North. The dearth of labor in Cochinchina prompted the French to recruit a work force from Tonkin, which was always overpopulated. French exploitation of workers and efforts to recruit workers in Tonkin to meet labor demands in Cochinchina and French possessions in the Pacific by impressing tax delinquents finally led to the assassination of Bazin, a French recruiter, in a Hanoi park in February 1929, touching off a series of arrests and repressive measures from French authorities.

To generate more revenue, the French legalized drinking and opium smoking. The sale of alcoholic beverages and opium, however, was a monopoly of the colonial government. Customs personnel, therefore, clamped down on moonshiners and those who dealt in alcohol and opium without a license. Though not prohibited, gambling during that period was not as widespread and open as it was in 1953-54, partly because of general poverty and partly because Vietnamese society was rather conservative.

Social stratification and class discrimination, once benign, now became accentuated. This was because the French had always wanted Vietnamese society to be deeply class-conscious. The old social hierarchy of "scholars-farmers-craftsmen-merchants" underwent some change which found the merchants prevailing over the farmers. A new class, the soldiers, had been added to the bottom rung of the social ladder; since they came mostly from the ranks of the illiterate peasantry, the soldiers were the most spurned by society. Men of letters still retained their preeminent rank although true scholars were becoming rare. During this transitional period, people with an elementary or junior high education were all called educated. That was the educational level required to qualify for a low or middle-level civil servant job, which was socially quite prestigious. Therefore, academic degrees, especially those conferred by French schools in country or in France, were the criteria by which a person's worth was evaluated, the crown of social success. Vietnamese were conscious of the prestige and distinction of French schools with French teachers and an all-French curriculum. In time, they assumed that there was a difference in value between the diplomas earned in French schools and those conferred by Vietnamese institutions although both curricula were practically the same. This prejudice pushed the snobbish and the well-to-do to send their children abroad, especially to France, or at least to local French schools to complete their education.

As for religion, Christianity gradually gained ascendency from the support of French authorities as well as from its own organizational success. Though much less numerous than Buddhists, the Roman Catholics constituted the most powerful community in Vietnam, especially in the North. For their part, the more numerous Buddhists were losing ground because of their inability to unite into a national religious organization and the fact that Buddhism became increasingly riddled by heresy and superstition.

In late 1944 and early 1945, a terrible famine struck North Vietnam causing more than a million deaths. This came as a result of floods and the fact that the peasants had been ordered by the French government to reduce their rice crop in order to plant jute which was being sought by the Japanese. Though causing the worst misery, the famine instigated no popular revolt, a fact that testified to the French success in paralyzing Vietnamese society in a systematic way. French authorities took no action to organize or encourage relief. Meanwhile, of the huge rice surplus available in the South, the French redistributed only a tiny portion, more for propaganda than for humanitarian purposes.

In short, Vietnamese society at the end of World War II, after French rule had been suddenly terminated by the Japanese, displayed all the signs of stagnancy and backwardness. Still laboring under traditionalism and the vestiges of Chinese influence, this society was suffering from the half-hearted reforms and colonial policies of French rule. The process of eradicating ancient Chinese influence and reforming society on a modern pattern had just begun and resulted in many dislocations. This was a transitional period during which the old evil was yet to be replaced by the new good and the new evil had already arrived to add to the old one.

Nationalists who were fighting against the French were all patriotic, but they lacked political shrewdness and experience. Premature emergence from the underground also doomed their activities to failure. They were even betrayed by Vietnamese who shared their anti-colonialist stance but not their political ideas, then also by the Communists who sold them out to the French. Finally, those who had allied themselves with the Japanese against the French ended up being betrayed, too. This hopeless situation lasted until the Japanese defeat. By that time, nationalist parties had been so depleted of talent and leadership that they were unable to take advantage of the political vacuum and seize power. Their inaction gave the Communist Viet Minh a chance to prevail on the people's patriotism and win national independence. Cunningly concealing their true nature and posing as nationalists, the Communists had managed to win the prime sympathy of the people.

Contact With Communism

The Indochinese Communist Party (ICP) was founded in 1930. When the Viet Minh, its frontal organization, seized power on 19 August 1945, the overwhelming majority of Vietnamese had only a vague idea of Communism.

Of particular significance at this juncture, most Vietnamese at heart seemed to consider the Viet Minh as just another nationalist group with a different organization and policy.

The psychology of the Vietnamese people at that time was one of yearning for national independence. At any price, Vietnam had to be returned to Vietnamese rule; political persuasion only came second. Ho Chi Minh's skill was in his ability to exploit popular hatred of French colonialism and his manipulation of nationalists. In late 1945, therefore, he disbanded the Indochinese Communist Party to the confusion of domestic and world opinion. In fact, he had shrewdly prepared for an eventual showdown with the French that required total popular support for success.

In the rush of events that preceded the eruption of the resistance war against the French on 19 December 1946, the Viet Minh also astutely instituted some long due social reforms. They advanced a program of anti-feudalism and anti-colonialism. Feudalism, they maintained, was at the source of all social evils and had to be destroyed first; then came the fight against colonialism. The anti-feudalism campaign sought primarily to demolish all monarchical vestiges in Vietnam and eliminate the old ruling class.[3] Popular sentiment, however, was only lukewarm toward this effort. The majority of the Vietnamese people only saw the French as the main enemy to eliminate. Their spirit and courage were evident at the oubreak of the war, when the people of Hanoi organized themselves into self-defense groups and battled the French from house to house for one month. The Viet Minh government and army, meanwhile, had withdrawn from the capital city before fighting broke out to establish a defense line in the higlands.

The call to join the Viet Minh army and fight for national salvation during 1947-50 was enthusiastically supported by many men from the middle

---

[3] Pham Quynh, a prominent scholar, and Ngo Dinh Khoi were both assassinated during the process.

class. Many of them had risen to the positions of battalion and regimental commanders in Vo Nguyen Giap's army. But most of these people were subsequently purged when the Viet Minh, in a move toward socialism, began to systematically eliminate the rich, the large landowners, and the petty bourgeoisie through the device of class struggle and land reform.

Vietnamese from all walks of life, with the exception of destitute peasants and workers, were greatly disappointed. They felt that the Viet Minh had betrayed them after enticing them to join the resistance. Driven by patriotic ardor and zeal, they had never thought of themselves as belonging to the classes destined to be eliminated.

From the very beginning of this watershed event, the poor farm workers had gained ascendency as they were entrusted with leadership positions in villages, districts, and provinces against the will of members of other classes. But as the new leaders exercised power under the aegis of the Lao Dong (Communist) Party, opposition and criticism began to evaporate. This change in the power structure of society entailed drastic change in the role of the Vietnamese women. Heretofore, utterly dependent in a traditional way, they had now emerged as men's equal partners in all aspects of social endeavor.

Living under Viet Minh control, Vietnamese from disfavored classes suffered from a radical change in social values. Being mostly city dwellers, they had been brought to the countryside by the war. The Viet Minh's scorched-earth policy had deprived them of economic advantages, and in a sense, this had the good effect of bridging the gap between city and countryside.

However, beginning in 1950, and especially during 1951, when the Viet Minh launched a forceful campaign of class struggle under the land rent reduction program, the illusion of class harmony was quickly fading away and yielded to the stark fact that only one class, the class of landless peasants and workers, was to remain and that all others were to vanish regardless of their contributions to the resistance. For this reason, a number of nationalists began to leave the Viet Minh zone for the cities, especially after the political reincarnation of ex-Emperor Bao Dai who was being used as a rallying point for those disillusioned with the Viet Minh. Except for Central Vietnam where royalist sentiments were still strong, Bao Dai failed to attract enough ralliers elsewhere because of his pro-French stance. Nevertheless, he was the only straw for all nationalists to cling to while they waited for a chance to revive their cause. The only alternative would have been capitulation and complete subservience to the French.

The socialist transformation carried out by the Viet Minh was forceful and rigid in North and Central Vietnam. But in the South, it had been so mild that in 1954 when the Geneva Agreements were concluded there were no significant popular grievances against Communist policy except for a few die-hard nationalists and members of the Cao Dai, Hoa Hao and Binh Xuyen, who had been frustrated with the treachery of the Communists Viet Minh.

The French defeat at Dien Bien Phu in May 1954 led rapidly to the signing of the Geneva Cease-Fire Agreement in late July 1954. Vietnam, was temporarily divided at the 17th parallel into two zones, North and South, pending the holding of general elections to reunify the country. The North was under a Communist government led by Ho Chi Minh while the South, nominally under the leadership of ex-Emperor Bao Dai and a nationalist government headed by Prime Minister Ngo Dinh Diem, still labored under French political and military control.

In its first steps toward regaining full sovereignty, South Vietnam had become an arena for the infighting of several opposing forces. First there was the French influence, which was exerted by the presence of the French High Commissioner and the French Expeditionary Corps. Then there were pro-French groups who worked with the French to promote their material interests as well as dubious political aims. In direct opposition to the French, there were the Communist Viet Minh who, despite their regrouping to the North, still enjoyed tremendous popular sympathy; their infrastructure and capability to return constituted perhaps the most obvious threat. All forces of nationalist persuasion wanted to take advantage of the temporary partition and the impending withdrawal of French forces to forge an independent course for the building of a non-Communist nation. To achieve this, they, who had never lived in harmony with each other, had to find a common rallying point.

In the midst of these searing conflicts, the stabilization of South Vietnam required immediate solutions in several areas. There were social differences to patch up; there was the shaky old order to unravel while a foundation for new values had yet to become firm; there was the need for rehabilitating a countryside torn up by war in addition to satisfying a Westernized pluralistic city population which was forever clamoring for more benefits; finally, there were the smoldering embers of discrimination to be mitigated, and this encompassed almost the entire fabric of society. Even though the American involvement was most opportune, the initial stages of South Vietnam's struggle to stand on its own feet were beset with obstacles. The extent of the nation-building effort and American assistance, the gravity of social problems, and the issues of government and leadership will be the topics of discussion in the following chapters.

CHAPTER II

The Consolidation of South Vietnam

The Preliminary Conditions

In the aftermath of the Dien Bien Phu debacle on 7 May 1954, the balance of power in Vietnam tilted heavily toward the Communist Viet Minh. Faced with increasing pressure, the French High Command in Indochina decided to abandon the Red River Delta and to redeploy its forces for the defense of the Hanoi and Hai Phong areas and Route No. 5 which was the vital corridor linking these two important cities. This audacious decision and its speedy execution were a military success in that it released enough forces to provide the reinforcements required for the defense of these last French enclaves in North Vietnam.

On the other hand this withdrawal of French forces brought about momentous consequences. The loyal population of the Red River Delta, who had rallied for many years to the Bao Dai government and fought against the Communist Viet Minh, suddenly found themselves vulnerable. As the last units of the French Union forces destroyed bridges and roads behind them, the Nationalist people in the provinces of Ninh Binh, Nam Dinh, Ha Nam and Hung Yen hastily began their flight toward Hanoi. Their exit was far from being easy. First, the event was totally unexpected; except for high-ranking military authorities, few could have envisaged such a rapid defeat. Nobody in fact had been prepared for this departure. Second, all lines of communication had been cut off. The worst difficulties were experienced by the people of the two Roman Catholic dioceses of Phat Diem and Bui Chu, the most remote areas which were also the most actively anti-Communist being abandoned.

The Geneva Agreements of 20 July 1954 eventually resolved the military predicament of the French and provided the people of Vietnam the opportunity of choosing between the two newly divided zones. A moratorium was subsequently implemented during which Communist forces took over areas still under French control. It was also the period of authorized evacuation for the population of both zones; for the Hanoi-Haiphong area, this moratorium was set at 300 days.

During the first few days of this evacuation, the Communists virtually took no action. People from the southern Delta of North Vietnam were moving in droves into the Hanoi-Haiphong area. In spite of the impassable roads and bridges, they kept moving by all available means: walking, wading across rice fields and rivulets, and boating down rivers or along the coast to Haiphong if they lived near the sea.

After a few days had passed Communist authorities realized the complications that were being caused by these mass movements. They began to interfere, first with mild measures, then with sterner and increasingly violent actions. Many villages and towns were cordoned off and placed under close surveillance; people were allowed to move only if they had special passes. Despite this, the refugees managed to flee under cover of darkness or by other surreptitious ways. Their immediate goal was to reach the Hanoi-Haiphong area; from there evacuation to South Vietnam became almost a certainty.

Among the groups that were leaving, the most cohesive and best organized were perhaps the Roman Catholics; led by determined priests they would not hesitate to use violence to clear their way. Some, however, were less successful. As commander of an armor unit stationed on Route No. 5 at that time, I personally observed the plight of one such community nearby, the Catholic village of Kim Bich, about 10 km north of Hai Duong.[1] All the villagers wanted to leave but the cordon of Viet Minh guerrillas was too tight. To deliver them, I had to maneuver my armor unit through the cordon. Without my armored vehicles, it would have been impossible for these villagers to break through and leave. This occurred just one week after cease-fire day.

---

[1] This commander was Nguyen Duy Hinh. In 1972 he was promoted to Major General, as Commander of the 3d ARVN Division, and is the coauthor of this monograph.

Even in the areas under the control of French and Vietnamese forces, the departure of the people, especially government officials, was not easy. At that time the Communists had their cadres and agents deployed almost everywhere, even in the inner cities. Many households were visited by cadres who advised against leaving or threatened to keep them from leaving. For many people, therefore, the departure from Hanoi or Haiphong had to be carried out discreetly. Properties and houses could not be sold or belongings carried away openly. Preparations for the exodus had to be made to appear as if people were intent on staying. The more discreet the preparations, the better the chance of successful departure.

Against units of the National Army of Vietnam, the Communists implemented a cunning scheme. Early on the morning of cease-fire day, most remote outposts and installations were besieged, not by Communist forces, but by groups of women, young and old. They had come, they said, to celebrate the cease-fire and to invite our troops to leave their units now that hostilities were over. Even troop movements were delayed by groups of these women. Many convoys were forced to a halt and a number of men left their units. Furthermore, during the time they waited for their departure by ship to the South, many of our wavering soldiers began to desert. Either they had received news from their families being held as hostages or visits by relatives who, under Communist coercion, were begging them to stay. Although commanders had tried to evacuate dependents along with the troops, they could not help those soldiers whose families lived in remote areas. This accounted for an unusually high desertion rate among soldiers prior to the evacuation from the North.

Eventually, as a result of American and French relief efforts, nearly a million Vietnamese located in the North had made their way to the South by planes or by ships. Had it not been for the obstructions and ploys of Communist authorities, the exodus would have been considerably larger.

What had impelled these many North Vietnamese to leave their places of birth and accept an uncertain future? Vietnamese had always been

strongly attached to their native land. It was where their ancestors
had been buried, where their relatives lived, and where they maintained
a home, a garden, or a ricefield which might have taken generations to
acquire. Their departure in many cases had been fraught with pain and
innumerable hazards. Even those who had collaborated with the Viet Minh
in fighting against the French for several years now resigned themselves
to follow the refugees's steps, aware that they were going to live under
a regime which was still largely pro-French.

There were several reasons for this mass exodus. The most powerful
driving force was obviously the determination to fight Communism which
had been acquired through experience with the Viet Minh. If during the
early years of 1945-48 the entire Vietnamese people had seemed to be
carried away by patriotic ardor, it was because the Viet Minh had
carefully concealed their Marxist nature. But in later years, after
the Viet Minh nationalistic mask had dropped, many people realized they
had been duped by the most blatant scheme of exploitation and deceit.
The resistance against the French had given the Vietnamese Communist
Party its supreme status. From 1950 on, Vietnamese Communist leaders
felt so reassured of popular support that they embarked on a class
struggle movement in many areas even though, in Vietnamese society,
there were no serious class distinctions or conflicts. The middle class
and petty bourgeois, though not rich, felt themselves threatened despite
the fact that they had sacrificed a great deal for the cause of the
resistance.

For those who had connections with nationalist parties, past
experience was even more traumatic. Their cooperation with the Viet
Minh in an anti-French coalition, called Vietnam Revolutionary League
from 1942 to 1945, only strengthened the position of the Viet Minh,
which was an offspring of the Indochinese Communist Party. Nationalist
leaders who subsequently joined Ho Chi Minh's coalition government in
late 1945 found themselves used and betrayed. A civil war, therefore,
broke out between Viet Minh and Nationalist forces and continued until
well after French forces had moved into North Vietnam in 1946 to replace
Nationalist Chinese forces. The Viet Minh then collaborated with the
French to eliminate their enemies. For several months, bloody battles

raged in the highland provinces of Vinh Yen, Phuc Yen, Phu Tho, Viet Tri, and Lao Kay during which the Viet Minh army systematically annihilated armed elements of the Viet Nam Quoc Dan Dang. In Haiphong and Lang Son, the Viet Minh mercilessly crushed the Vietnam Cach Mang Dong Minh Hoi, their allies during maquis days. Then, they attacked and destroyed the Dai Viet strongholds in the Hon Gay-Cam Pha area. By June 1946, all nationalist forces had been driven out into southern China. Finally, the Viet Minh moved rapidly to take over the headquarters of these parties in Hanoi in June 1946. Their subsequent hunt for remaining Nationalist elements in Hanoi and the provinces resulted in tortures and executions that were to remain forever a nationalist nightmare. All these events demonstrated that Nationalists and Communists simply could not coexist. They also explained why the nationalist hatred toward Communists had been so deep-seated over the years.

The love for freedom in general was also a strong motivating force behind the exodus of Northerners. Vietnamese are basically liberty-loving people. They tenaciously fought against foreign domination because of their ingrained spirit of freedom and independence. Cognizant of this sensitivity, even French administrators had left the material and spiritual life of Vietnamese families and villages largely undisturbed. Therefore, except for superficial changes in towns and cities, under French rule the overwhelming majority of Vietnamese still retained their own way of life. Rural peasants continued to enjoy a physically harsh but spiritually unfettered and free existence. This freedom to work, to enjoy the fruits of one's labor, and to live as one pleased was gradually curtailed and life was increasingly regimented under a Viet Minh regime.

Granted that a nation fighting for its independence had to accept sacrifice and some abridgment of liberties. But it was a different matter when these restrictions paved the way for authoritarian rule. Several well-to-do citizens offered their properties in support of the government, feeding troops, and sponsoring organizations, but this inevitable contribution was anything but voluntary. There was no longer any freedom of thought because all imprudent expressions or grievances were automatically regarded as traitorous or reactionary behavior.

Communist fund drives and subtle exploitation under the cloak of resistance against the French failed to cover up their ulterior motives and long-range plans. The situation was such that most citizens with wealth and properties had to relinquish everything and leave. Impoverished by Viet Minh exploitation, the poor became poorer and would have fled also if they had had the means.

In spite of the regime's protestations of all sorts of freedoms, the actions and policies of the Viet Minh showed that freedom of religion was not guaranteed. The Buddhists, always lacking in cohesion and organization, remained silent. But the Catholic community, which was well organized and led, had come into conflict with the Viet Minh from the very first days of the "August 1945 Revolution." These conflicts had become more and more serious although Ho Chi Minh was constantly proclaiming freedom of religion. During the war, wherever French forces moved in, Catholic villages that had been resisting Viet Minh authorities in isolation began to cooperate in the pacification efforts of the Nationalist government and the French High Command. When this pacification spread to the coastal provinces of Nam Dinh and Ninh Binh, the two largest catholic dioceses of North Vietnam, Bui Chu and Phat Diem, became instantly anti-Communist strongholds. Under the leadership of two prominent bishops, Pham Ngoc Chi and Le Huu Tu, both dioceses organized their own combat villages and formed their own self-defense forces. When the country was later partitioned, it was no wonder that most evacuees consisted of Catholics. They had fought atheism and were determined to seek freedom of religion.

When North Vietnamese in search of freedom arrived in South Vietnam in 1954, the naive and accommodating attitude of most Southerners toward the Communists caught them by surprise. Apparently, the Viet Minh had not yet revealed their true character to the local population. It could be that since they were far removed from their main base in North Vietnam, the Viet Minh had not firmly established themselves, and their forces had not enjoyed the military and political strength that they had in the North. In South Vietnam, the catch phrase advocated by the Viet Minh to enlist popular support had not gone beyond "National unity to fight the French and regain national independence." The bloody socialist transformation that the Viet Minh were implementing elsewhere in the country was not conspicuous; at least, it had not been perceived as keenly by Southerners as it had been by Northerners.

However, among the upper class of South Vietnamese society, among members of nationalist parties, and among religious sects, anti-Communist feelings were particularly strong. For these people, the true dictatorial and bloodthirsty character of the Communist Viet Minh had revealed itself fairly early. In 1945, the scramble for leadership of the resistance movement against the French had brought to light the many wiles of Tran Van Giau and later of Nguyen Binh, both of the Viet Minh. Following the Japanese capitulation, Nationalist leaders promptly joined forces and took over leadership of the movement in Saigon, but for the purpose of uniting forces against the French they later yielded leadership to Tran Van Giau. In their jockeying for power, the Viet Minh did not hesitate to liquidate any adversaries they deemed dangerous. Bui Quang Chieu, founder of the Constitutionalist Party, Vo Van Nga, leader of the Party for Independence, and Nguyen Van Sam, the Imperial Delegate to Cochinchina, were all assassinated. In Hue, the Viet Minh killed the scholar Pham Quynh and Ngo Dinh Khoi, Ngo Dinh Diem's eldest brother, both from the former Bao Dai government and dignitaries with prestige in their times. The Viet Minh did not even spare their own comrades who happened to have divergent views; they killed Ta Thu Thau, for example, who was leader of the Trotskyist Struggle Group. This reign of terror eventually brought about the collapse of the nationalist movement in the South and gave the Viet Minh the indisputable leadership position in the resistance movement.

To the Cao Dai and Hoa Hao sects and the Binh Xuyen organization, the Viet Minh initially showed some restraint, but still tried to dominate them. Eventually, however, when cooperation had proved all but impossible, Huynh Phu So, the Hoa Hao spiritual leader, was ambushed and killed. Fearing the same fate, the Cao Dai Pope, Pham Cong Tac, had to flee to Cambodia. As for the Binh Xuyen, after collaborating with the Viet Minh for some time, they, too, realized the threat to their own existence and switched allegiance to the French. From then on, it could be said that all Cao Dai and Hoa Hao adherents and members of the Binh Xuyen were the most dedicated anti-Communists of South Vietnam.

When South Vietnam emerged as a nation south of the 17th parallel, it was built on a large anti-Communist base. This base consisted of a million North Vietnamese refugees to include families of military and civil servants, over three million Cao Dai and Hoa Hao adherents, and other military and paramilitary forces. South Vietnamese society at that time could be divided into three significant categories: a small minority with Communist connection and underground Communist cadres, who were hostile to the Nationalist cause; the urban middle class whose social status made them incompatible with a Communist regime; and the rural peasantry which was uncommitted but malleable. The conditions were therefore opportune for the forging of a strong anti-Communist regime. But much seemed to depend on how the South Vietnamese government proceeded and whether this government could demonstrate its usefulness to the people.

Nationalism or the Nationalist cause upon which the Republic of Vietnam was being built was conceived as an antithesis to international Communism and as an ideological tool for motivation. The preservation of Vietnamese traditions, the maintenance of what remained of the Vietnamese heritage after nearly a century of French rule and nine years of destructive war and economic development, were promoted as strong incentives for the nation-building effort. South Vietnam certainly was not lacking in natural resources. With time and devotion, it should be able to heal all wounds of the past and become a strong, viable nation.

If Communist North Vietnam had the support of international Communism, South Vietnam was also enjoying increasing American support. A clear proof of this was the U.S. relief given to Northern refugees who were resettling in the South. The U.S. also refused to be a signatory party to the Geneva Agreements, which was another indication of U.S. commitment to the Nationalist cause. As tension increased during the Cold War that pitted the United States against the Soviet Union and especially after the Communist take-over of mainland China and the invasion of South Korea, there was no doubt that the United States had hardened its line against Communist expansion. With American support, South Vietnam appeared to have an excellent opportunity for success.

But South Vietnam's path was full of difficulties and hazards. The difficulties lay in the ravages caused by war, the divided allegiances of a people who seemed not easily amenable to a common purpose, and the necessity to maintain security and political stability during the nation-building effort. The hazards were primarily in the two-year period immediately following the partition of Vietnam and prior to unification through general elections. But since conditions were favorable for survival, the anti-Communist elements in South Vietnam nurtured the hope that under the U.S. protective shield, their new nation could be built into a durable anti-Communist bastion of the Free World in Southeast Asia. In the tense atmosphere of the mid-50's this was also the policy pursued with conviction by the United States in this part of the world.

Building Strength and A National Cause

One result of the 1954 Geneva Agreements was the creation of two Vietnams antagonistic to each other. When they came to take control of Hanoi after eight years of absence from the city, Ho Chi Minh, his government, and the Workers' (Communist) Party undoubtedly enjoyed tremendous political advantages. Having driven out the French and won back independence they were now basking in glory as the indisputable champion of the national cause in the eyes of many North Vietnamese people. After the last French units had withdrawn from Haiphong, North Vietnam was in perfect control of its own destiny. Eight years of war had thoroughly trained and prepared the North Vietnamese civil and military machinery to assume new endeavors. Though deprived of the manpower and skills that nearly a million people, or 17% of its total work force, had taken with them, the North could still make use of the considerable amount of property they left behind. To the world, and especially to the Communist bloc and the emerging nations of the Third World, North Vietnam was the prestigious hero of the resistance, a fact that seemed to diminish the status of South Vietnam and prompted outside observers to doubt its chances of survival.

Indeed, stability, the primary condition that South Vietnam needed for its survival was still a matter of conjecture. Long accustomed to existing in the shadow of the French, this part of the country emerged utterly unprepared to stand on its own feet. The antiquated, French-dominated administration was filled with people who had no understanding of the impending ideological struggle and had never been given a chance to make decisions for themselves. It was highly problematic that this administration could carry out new policies that required both ideological struggle and nation-building at the same time. Though numerous, nationalist factions and organizations were yet to show their ability to create strength through unity; if anything, they were already showing signs of divisiveness. It seemed that their leaders had learned nothing from their years of struggle with the Viet Minh, and popular confidence in their talents and prestige was tenuous at best. Such was the general situation in the South when Mr. Ngo Dinh Diem was appointed by Chief of State Bao Dai to serve as Prime Minister with full political and military powers.

This situation was both dark and difficult, especially for a new Prime Minister who, though enjoying personal prestige, had no real power base and was not supported by the French. This situation required first and foremost that he have a strong government and a unified, trustworthy army. But the Army was against him because it was led by pro-French generals and officers who had been appointed, supported, and commanded by the French. The police and security forces refused to take orders from him because law enforcement had been entrusted by the Chief of State to the armed Binh Xuyen bandits, who were now controlling it with a free hand. Mr. Diem's desire to rally nationalist forces behind him also ran counter to the selfish interests of the armed religious sects. Both the Cao Dai and Hoa Hao had carved out their own empires and were protecting them with jealousy. The French themselves were unwilling to relinquish their colonial holdings. The French Expeditionary forces had no intention of leaving Indochina, and French capitalists, who controlled banks, factories, and plantations, were naturally the last ones who desired to see French influence decline. Vietnamese politicians of Bao Dai's regime, who had been accustomed to fishing in troubled water and holing themselves up in ivory towers to bide their time, had all the less intention to cooperate with Mr. Diem after judging the situation as being too difficult. Meanwhile, nationalist parties, perhaps still stunned by events and most of all by the Communist victory, failed to contribute anything significant.

The only hope for Mr. Diem, therefore, lay in the popular masses who had suffered the most from the vicissitudes of the war, the North Vietnamese refugees who were looking forward to a fresh start in the South, and the rank and file of the National Armed Forces who were genuinely expecting strong measures from the government. These were probably the most positive forces on which Mr. Diem could rely in the murky situation of South Vietnam in late 1954.

Any nationalist government intent on rebuilding South Vietnam at that time could not fail to come to grips with a number of urgent problems. The first priority task, which was essential for the survival of the regime, was gaining full control of the army and rallying the autonomous armed factions that were defying governmental authority. No less important was the need to create internal unity, a common purpose and maintain law and order which were all necessary for the normal functioning of the state. Furthermore, government would succeed only if it could find a worthy national cause to vie with North Vietnam and with which the people could identify. This cause was none other than gaining full independence, that is, freedom from French dominance and building an effective, popularly accepted form of government.

Prime Minister Ngo Dinh Diem, even though cloistered in his palace, had the courage to reject compromise and to take firm actions toward fulfilling his objectives. He embarked on solving domestic problems first. His opponents were numerous and openly hostile to him. General Nguyen Van Hinh, the Chief of the General Staff of the National Army, declared openly that he needed only to pick up the telephone to unleash a coup d'etat; the Binh Xuyen, the Cao Dai, and the Hoa Hao were all proving very unfriendly. Unable to solve all the problem at the same time, Mr. Diem tackled them one by one.

The first and urgent task was to replace General Hinh while maintaining friendly relations with the religious sects. General Hinh, the son of former Prime Minister Nguyen Van Tam, had been a major in the French Air Force, had French nationality, and was married to a French woman. Employed by the French and elevated by them to the top position of the National Army, General Hinh could not fail to serve French interests. The elimination of General Hinh, therefore, took on the added meaning of erasing French influence in the South Vietnamese armed forces.

The crisis came to a showdown early in September 1954, when Prime Minister Diem sent General Hinh to France on a military study mission. General Hinh refused to go, and from then on the conflict broke into the open. The Binh Xuyen, Cao Dai, and Hoa Hao joined forces to support General Hinh; they petitioned Chief of State Bao Dai to replace the Prime Minister. At this critical juncture, nine cabinet members tended their resignation; but Prime Minister Diem did not give up. He reshuffled his cabinet and, by financial rewards, was able to bring eight leaders of the Cao Dai and Hoa Hao into his government. In late September, a new development seemed to tip the balance in the Prime Minister's favor: the Cao Dai general, Trinh Minh The, rallied with all the troops under his command.

Despite this, it took Mr. Diem three months to settle the General Hinh affair. Finally, in the face of unambiguous American support for Mr. Diem, the French backed down. In mid-November 1954, heeding a call from the Chief of State, General Hinh set out for France; in Saigon, General Le Van Ty was appointed new Chief of the General Staff. This was the first step toward consolidating the South Vietnamese government; because of the dangers involved, it was probably Mr. Diem's first big victory.

During this period, the situation was far from being peaceful in Saigon and in the provinces. In Saigon itself, the Binh Xuyen was in firm control of the police and security forces. Police precincts stationed throughout the city were also Binh Xuyen fortresses. Gambling casinos, brothels, and opium dens that dotted the city were under their sponsorship. Two main Binh Xuyen business enterprises, the Dai The Gioi gambling casino and the Binh Khanh brothel, opened for business day and night and were prospering. The arrogance of the Binh Xuyen police, their aggressiveness, and overbearing attitude were everyday occurrences in the streets of Saigon. The people and soldiers of the National Army were enraged; they expected nothing less than a general clean-up of this gang of official bandits.

In the provinces north and southwest of the capital, the Cao Dai and Hoa Hoa armies were imposing their feudal rule. For much too long, while fighting the Viet Minh and maintaining control over vast regions, they had been unrestrained in their actions, exploiting, collecting taxes, and bullying the people. High-ranking Cao Dai and Hoa Hao officers, though commanding some following, were far from leading an honest and moral life. With their armed units these religious sects were able to control and rule large rural areas while the people silently suffered. Under such circumstances, eliminating these armed groups was only conforming to the will of the people.

Having gained control of the National Army, Prime Minister Diem turned to his next task, that of eliminating the "feudal lords." Instead of doing it in one swift action, he skillfully maneuvered to create division among them, bribing some to pit them against others. His tactic was to clip their wings one by one in order to minimize losses. As a result of his maneuvers, in January 1955, two Hoa Hao groups rallied to the government: Colonel Nguyen Van Hue, General Tran Van Soai's Chief of Staff, with 3,500 men; and Major Nguyen Day with 1,500 men. Then, in late January 1955, Cao Dai general, Trinh Minh The turned over the remainder of his army. On 13 February 1955, his black shirt brigade, 5,000 strong, paraded in front of the diplomatic corps in Saigon, marking an undeniable triumph for Prime Minister Diem and for all of South Vietnam. For his loyalty, Trinh Minh The was immediately appointed a Brigadier General in the National Army.

The first three months of 1955, therefore, consisted of governmental maneuverings and machinations by the dissident groups. Though joined in a formal unified front against Mr. Diem, the religious sects and the Binh Xuyen failed to forge a true alliance. At the end of February 1955,

Cao Dai general, Nguyen Thanh Phuong, spokesman of this unified front, also rallied to the government with his army.

Thus, the only remaining opponent to the government was the Binh Xuyen, but, for obvious reasons, Prime Minister Diem was not anxious to gain their allegiance. In January 1955, in a drive to eliminate social vices, the government refused to renew the licenses of the Dai The Gioi gambling casino and the Binh Khang brothel. It was obvious that the conflict with the Binh Xuyen was becoming critical.

In late March 1955 the first important firefight broke out between government troops and the Binh Xuyen at the Saigon Police Headquarters; both sides sustained casualties. The French High Commissioner, General Paul Ely, intervened to prevent the National Army from attacking the Binh Xuyen. French forces were also deployed in blocking positions. They cut off supplies to the National Army while abetting the Binh Xuyen and allowing them to move and reinforce key areas.

The crisis in Saigon deepened. Several important cabinet ministers resigned, including Foreign Minister Tran Van Do and Defense Minister Ho Thong Minh. While the French almost openly supported the anti-government faction, the American position remained equivocal. In the face of this impasse, Prime Minister Diem decided to act forcefully.

On 28 April 1955, Army units launched a concerted attack on the Binh Xuyen with Trinh Minh The's brigade in the vanguard. After two days of fighting, all Binh Xuyen forces were driven out of the city. Forced out of the Saigon area, the remnants of the Binh Xuyen went into hiding in the Rung Sat, a swampy mangrove near the sea, southeast of the capital. A few months later, surrounded and battered by the National Army and demoralized by privation, and disease, the Binh Xuyen began to disintegrate and surrendered. Le Van Vien, their leader and some of his henchmen fled to France.

Actions against the Binh Xuyen chagrined Chief of State Bao Dai. Overplaying his hand he summoned Prime Minister Diem and the Chief of the General Staff, General Le Van Ty, to France for consultation. Both simply refused to comply with his order. It was all too apparent that the power of Bao Dai as an absentee chief of state began to evaporate once the United States threw its full support behind Prime Minister

Diem. On the other hand, the once-secret desire of the French to obstruct the consolidation of the new South Vietnamese government by encouraging the Binh Xuyen and religious sects also came out into the open. It was, therefore, no surprise that Bao Dai was later removed and the French asked to leave.

As for the Cao Dai sect, after the rallying of Generals Trinh Minh The and Nguyen Thanh Phuong and their forces, its strength had practically vanished. His problem with the Cao Dai now being political in nature, Prime Minister Diem applied an indirect tactic. In October 1955, Cao Dai general, Nguyen Thanh Phuong took his own troops to Tay Ninh to eliminate the dissident elements of his own sect. Pope Pham Cong Tac, accused of obscurantism, was deposed and fled to Cambodia, where he remained until his death. Unlike the Cao Dai, the Hoa Hao forces in the Mekong Delta were strong and more obstinate. To subdue them, Army units launched a large-scale operation in early June 1955 which forced five Hoa Hao battalions to surrender at Cai Von, near Can Tho. A Hoa Hao chieftain, General Nguyen Giac Ngo, also surrendered shortly thereafter, but General Tran Van Soai, alias Nam Lua, massed his forces near the Cambodian border for a showdown with government troops. Overwhelmed, General Soai, along with General Nguyen Van Hinh and General Nguyen Van Vy who had been sent back by Bao Dai to organize the fighting, was forced to flee into Cambodia. Early the following year, General Soai capitulated. Hoa Hao remnants now consisted of guerrilla bands under the command of General Le Quang Vinh, alias Ba Cut. In April 1956, Ba Cut was captured in an ambush, and after trial by a court-martial, was executed in Can Tho on 13 June 1956.

While endeavoring to unify nationalist forces, the Ngo Dinh Diem government also acted to regain full national sovereignty. This was an important move, especially since North Vietnam under the leadership of Ho Chi Minh had showed that it was independent. South Vietnam could not afford to be second in the eyes of the people, who wanted complete independence and the removal of all colonial vestiges. It was also a matter of prestige for South Vietnam as a newcomer in the community of nations. This competition for popular standing and national prestige was hardly possible with the continued presence of a French High Commissioner and the French Expeditionary Corps. Furthermore, when France signed the Geneva Agreements, she had pledged to withdraw from Indochina. Therefore, when the United States proceeded to urge France to return all sovereign powers to the South Vietnamese government, much to her regret, she had no choice but to comply. Since September 1954, the court system, national police, and civilian aeronautics had already been turned over to Vietnamese authorities. Then, at the end of 1954, after an economic and financial agreement, the Bank of Indochina and other French financial institutions were disbanded. The National Bank of Vietnam was created and began operation in early 1955. A few days later, the commercial port of Saigon also came under Vietnamese control.

Up to this point, everyone could see that the Ngo Dinh Diem government had achieved considerable progress, and no one could have any doubt about the positive course that South Vietnam was taking. Prime Minister Diem, whose resolve was now well-known, continued to press for full sovereignty. By the end of 1955, the French High Command had left Saigon, and all remaining French Union forces had regrouped to a transit station at Vung Tau. The General Staff of the Vietnamese National Army, now weaned from dependence on the French High Command, was prepared to carry out programs of reorganization and training with the assistance of the United States Training Relations and Instruction Mission (TRIM).

In late 1955, as if to sweep away the last vestiges of colonialism, the South Vietnamese government began to tackle the problem of French nationality. At this time a fairly large number of Vietnamese government officials and military officers had French nationality. Each individual concerned was given six months to decide on his nationality after which time no one with French nationality would be allowed to serve in the Vietnamese national government. Generals Tran Van Don and Tran Van Minh, Ambassador Tran Van Chuong, and several others chose to relinquish French citizenship. On this occasion, many Vietnamese officers also parted with their French names. For the National Armed Forces, a new system of rank insignia was instituted to replace the old one of French origin. The French insignia burning ceremony, held at the

Joint General Staff headquarters, was a sensational occasion that excited the curiosity of the press and the people.

At the end of April 1956, after further requests by the South Vietnamese government, the last French forces left Vietnam, ending a long French military presence in the South. Relations with France were subsequently maintained on the diplomatic, economic, and cultural levels, the only relations that South Vietnam wanted to keep for its own benefit.

Prime Minister Diem's uncompromising attitude toward feudal warlordism and French dominance underlined his determination to erase all vestiges of the colonial past and steer the nation toward a new destiny. This could not be achieved as long as his leadership was handicapped. Some maintained that Mr. Ngo Dinh Diem had always had the ambition of becoming chief of state and had prepared plans to depose Bao Dai. While there was no evidence to substantiate this, by that time, Mr. Diem had unquestionably demonstrated that he was the leader the nation needed. There was no doubt that Bao Dai had lost all of his prestige with the people.

In his youth, when returning home from his studies in France in 1932, Bao Dai had nurtured the dream of modernizing the country for the benefit of his people. He had enjoyed some measure of respectability. But when confronted with French rejection of his reforms, he had resigned himself to the role of a figurehead. Besides, he was the descendent of a royal line that the people held responsible for France's subjugation of Vietnam.

He had let an opportunity to save his country slip away when the Japanese overthrew French rule on 9 March, 1945. The banner was then passed on to him, but he failed to act. His role was banished from history when in August 1945 the Viet Minh rose to power and he had to abdicate. For his acceptance to serve as Ho Chi Minh's adviser, the Communists lauded him as "patriotic" and "wise". But the Nationalists were distressed that he was not a person with a will to fight.

When the French realized that they could not win the military war against the Viet Minh, they looked for a figurehead for their "nationalist solution" experiment in hopes of diluting the ranks of resistance fighters. Bao Dai consented to play this role in 1949 after some of his conditions were met. But instead of taking advantage of the French impasse to work for the nationalist cause, he once again accepted the position of being a mere puppet. French authorities must have been reassured to see the Vietnamese chief of state spending most of his time on the French Riviera, leaving them a free hand to rule the new state as they wanted. His dissipated life forced him to accept money even from gangsters. That was how the Binh Xuyen had been put in charge of the Saigon police force. Bao Dai's fate was sealed when Prime Minister Diem ignored his summons after the disintegration of the Binh Xuyen.

On 7 July 1955, in a ceremony to commemorate the first anniversary of his government, Prime Minister Diem announced that a popular referendum would be held on 23 October of that year so that the people could choose their own form of government. By doing this, he had forced a popular choice between himself and ex-Emperor Bao Dai. The result of the referendum was a foregone conclusion. Given the people's attitude at that time, there was no need for any maneuverings on the part of Prime Minister Diem's supporters. On 26 October 1955 in a solemn ceremony, Mr. Ngo Dinh Diem declared South Vietnam a Republic, and officially assumed its first Presidency.

The downfall of Bao Dai enhanced the national cause and boosted President Diem's stature as a strong leader opposed to Ho Chi Minh. South Vietnam needed his leadership to become a viable nation. Mr. Diem's ascendency carried with it the significance of upholding nationalist beliefs, a severance of ties with the foreign-dominated past and complete secession from North Vietnam.

President Diem's successes had been much applauded. Only one year after assuming power as a handicapped Prime Minister trying to govern a war-torn and troubled country in the name of an absentee chief of state, he had emerged as President of a sovereign and orderly Republic. In conjunction with its efforts to regain sovereign powers and establish political stability, the Diem Administration also carried out several programs to strengthen national authority and control.

The 1954 Geneva Agreement had seen most Viet Minh forces and some of their ardent sympathizers regroup to North Vietnam. Simultaneously with efforts to eliminate rebellious sects, the South Vietnamese Army launched a series of operations to take over areas formerly under Viet Minh control such as Ca Mau, Xuyen Moc, Binh Dinh and Quang Ngai. Accompanying military forces were psychological warfare, medical, and civil action teams that endeavored to help the people and win their allegiance to the national cause.

With U.S. assistance, South Vietnamse armed forces began training and reorganizing. The Army formed infantry divisions which were trained and equipped to face open aggression from Communist North Vietnam. To meet the threat of insurgency from within, auxiliary and local forces were organized into the Civil Guard and Self-Defense Corps. To control Communist subversion and clandestine operations, a police and security network, including special security forces such as the Special Action Teams, was put into operation.

Emerging from difficult circumstances and responsible for a nation that was constantly facing a serious threat from the North, the South Vietnamese government was pursuing a twofold objective: to develop the national cause and to strengthen national defense. As part of his effort to promote the national cause after the Republic was formed, President Diem initiated the process of democratizing the nation. However, developing the strength for effective national defense was given the most emphasis and became the underlying principle of all national programs. The requirement for survival prevailed over all other considerations during the First Republic. This need to remain secure from the North Vietnamese threat became apparent in every program from information, propaganda and organization of the masses to the resettlement of refugees and economic and social development. Preoccupation with internal security and the survival of the regime eventually led President Diem to consolidate his own powers, despite the nation's democratic outlook. His centralization of authority and rigid leadership effectively made him an authoritarian ruler, a fact that dissatisfied nationalist factions and to which the United States took exception.

As part of the democratization process, five months after the birth of the Republic, a Constitutional Assembly was elected on 4 March 1956. Towards the end of 1956, on the first birthday of the young Republic, the Constitution of the Republic of Vietnam was proclaimed. This constitution lay the foundation for a Presidential system of government which instituted direct popular vote for the Presidency and gave the Executive branch more powers than the legislative or Judiciary. In due course, two Presidential elections were held, one in 1957 and the other in 1961, as well as two parliamentary elections in 1959 and 1963, with the Constitutional Assembly serving beyond its intended term.

Whether President Diem's political development process was flawed and whether one lauded or slighted his accomplishments was a matter of personal opinion. Most conceded, however, that his administration had at least brought about stability and a measure of law and order. This was essential not only to carry out the struggle against the Communists but also to reconstruct a country whose economy had been ravaged by war and whose political forces were immature, complex, and divided.

National reconstruction and economic development programs received a great deal of attention. With American assistance, North Vietnamese refugees and displaced persons in the South had been resettled or returned to their home villages within two years, 1955 and 1956. Several resettlement areas such as Cai San and Ho Noi, and pioneer farming projects began to prosper. Roads and bridges were rebuilt; the railroad link from Saigon to Quang Tri was reopened. The production of rice and other crops, cattle raising, and fishing were rapidly increasing. Rice production rose from 2.6 million metric tons in 1954 to 5 million tons in 1959 and rubber production from 51,000 to 79,000 tons during the same period. In 1960 South Vietnam was exporting 70,000 metric tons of rubber and 340,000 metric tons of rice.

A base was also laid for industrial development. In this connection, the South Vietnamese government had decided to cooperate with the private sector in order to stimulate and control development. Many small firms, therefore, proliferated and larger industries were founded as joint government-private ventures. Two industrial zones, the Saigon-Bien Hoa complex and the Nong Son-An Hoa area in Quang Nam Province, began to grow and expand. Vietnamese industry started producing textiles, sugar, glass, medicines, cement, and other consumer goods.

Building economic strength was pursued in conjunction with social progress in every aspect. Public health and education developed rapidly. The student population rose from 400,000 in 1956 to 1,500,000 in 1960 a near fourfold increase. In addition to the University of Saigon, two other universities, Hue and Dalat, were founded to promote higher education.

Embedded in most development programs was the underlying concern for national security. The resettlement and development patterns from 1955 to 1958 reflected the GVN plans to control insecure and remote border areas through farming projects, the building of pioneer roads and canals, and the creation of new provincial capitals and district towns. In addition to study projects in the Truong Son Cordillera, the GVN also devoted efforts to enlisting the cooperation of Montagnards and organizing the people elsewhere. When the Communists began their terrorist offensive, the GVN response was the agroville program. As Communist guerrilla warfare intensified, a large-scale pacification effort called the strategic hamlet program was initiated in 1961 and actively pursued during 1962.

Toward the middle of 1963, while the strategic hamlet program was showing signs of success in checking the growth of Communist insurgency in the rural areas, an urban religious crisis eventually led to the coup d'etat of 1 November 1963. President Ngo Dinh Diem and his brother-counselor Ngo Dinh Nhu, who masterminded several important programs, were killed. With the collapse of the First Republic went most of the accomplishments of the past nine years in the areas of nation-building and developing the strength to fight against Communism. The strategic hamlet program, which was at the core of the defense effort, met its rapid demise when members of the main rural defense force, the Republican Youth, hastily deserted their ranks for fear of reprisals because of their association with the fallen regime. The new leaders, meanwhile, had yet to conceive an alternate plan for the defense of the rural areas.

The death of President Diem ushered in an era of political instability in South Vietnam. Civilian and military governments surfaced and disappeared in rapid succession while religious and political groups jockeyed for power. Military leaders in the armed forces were affected by the national strife and became factional. Political disturbance and power struggles seemed to tear the fabric of South Vietnamese society. Taking advantage of this situation, North Vietnam stepped up its subversive efforts and infiltrated regular forces to join in the fight. From all indications, South Vietnam seemed ready to fall prey to a Communist military victory. This desperate situation compelled the United States to bomb North Vietnam and send troops to fight in South Vietnam in 1965.

With U.S. forces on South Vietnamese battlefields, the situation began to improve. After a long period of turmoil and factional bickerings, by June 1965, Lt. General Nguyen Van Thieu and Major General Nguyen Cao Ky had emerged at the head of a government dedicated to stabilization and progress.

About a year later, the same militant Buddhist group that had precipitated the events leading to President Diem's downfall began to demand a return to civilian rule. Under U.S. pressure, the military government decided upon a new course toward democracy. Avoiding the tight centralization of powers that had prevailed during the First Republic, the government broadened its base to include political parties and religious groups and instituted elections at the rice-roots level. But it seemed that to legitimize its existence, the new government also needed to be confirmed through general elections.

In September 1966, therefore, a Constitutional Assembly, the second one to date was elected. After the promulgation of a new constitution, a presidential election was conducted on 3 September 1967. The Nguyen Van Thieu-Nguyen Cao Ky ticket, which represented the military, won by a slight margin. These elections conferred a measure of legitimacy to the South Vietnamese government despite its military affiliation. Evidently religious groups and political parties had yet to prove themselves and in the situation of South Vietnam at that time, it appeared that the military was the only cohesive force capable of conducting the war against the Communists and establishing internal stability at the same time.

Concurrently, the United States continued to increase its military involvement and the situation was steadily improving with the expansion of the RVNAF and concerted pacification efforts. In the midst of

optimism and high expectations, the 1968 Tet General Offensive came as
a rude awakening to the urban people of South Vietnam. Towns and cities
that had been spared previously of war hazards were suddenly engulfed.
Realizing the far greater danger of a Communist victory, city people
began to shelter differences in opinion and join in the war effort by
enlisting in the military service or serving in People's Self-Defense
Forces.

South Vietnam in the aftermath of the Communist military defeat
during 1968 displayed all the signs of restored confidence and renewed
vitality. Spurred on by increased popular allegiance to the national
cause, the GVN pushed vigorously ahead with the rural pacification and
development program which soon brought the near totality of hamlets and
their population under governmental control. The national economy
rapidly recovered with increased rice production and the influx of larger
U.S. aid. Although inflation continued to boost consumer prices, its
pressure seemed to ease on the rural peasantry. The prospects for the
future never seemed so promising especially after the distribution of
free farmland to the landless peasants under the 1970 agrarian reform.

All this progress was interrupted by the Communist 1972 Easter Offensive which, despite its furor and destruction, failed to subdue South
Vietnam. Nevertheless, the nation began to doubt its capability of
survival without U.S. support. The Paris Agrement of January 1973 reinforced this doubt when South Vietnam was left to fend for itself alone.
With all U.S. combat troops now gone and U.S. aid reduced, South Vietnamese
felt vulnerable and less and less reassured of their chance of survival.
In the midst of these difficult times, South Vietnamese society, which
had never been united in the anti-Communist struggle, was sinking deeper
into division and selfishness. Internal strife and the threat of collapse
were also aggravating. The authority of government and national leaders
as well as popular faith sank to an all-time low. It was no longer possible
to mobilize the masses, and the survival strength of South Vietnam was
visibly on the decline with each new Communist attack.

Motivation of the People

The world-wide struggle against Communism, perhaps more than any other form of conflict, has pointed up the vital role of the people. The 1917 victory of the Russian Boloheviks depended mostly on techniques of mobilizing the masses. Mao Tse Tung's success in 1949 came only after the Chinese people had lost faith in the Nationalists and because the Communists had been able to gain control of the majority of the populace. In Vietnam, Ho Chi Minh's victory in the 1945-54 war against the French again seemed to demonstrate the merits of "people's war" which the Communists are still boasting.

The Vietnamese Communists claimed that their struggle in South Vietnam was based on the power of the people. In this strategy of subversion, therefore, politics was the basis for every action. Of necessity, military action was subordinated to political needs or used to exploit political gains. Violence was the means to reach political objectives.

As Hanoi's leaders saw it, people's war had three characteristics. First, it was a war waged by the entire people. In fact, the people were manipulated, exhorted, and deceived into joining the war effort. Since the people provided manpower and material resources, as the war grew in intensity, the Communists were able to sustain greater losses only through a merciless manipulation of the masses. Second, it was a total war, waged in every field of endeavor. But carrying the fight into all domains certainly created enormous difficulties for our enemy. Finally, because it depended so much on the people to grow and expand, it had to be a protracted war. Obviously, people could be organized and controlled only gradually and our enemy needed time to overcome the many problems occasioned by the war.

During the Vietnam War, therefore, winning the hearts and minds of the people was just as essential for the GVN as maintaining security. In practice, these two objectives were meshed together in many cases, and their pursuit overshadowed the purely economic development effort. All nationalist governments from Mr. Diem to Mr. Thieu were aware of the necessity to win the support of the people. It was obvious that with the people on our side we could create our own strength and drain the enemy's, by denying him the use of manpower and other resources. This would also provide the opportunity to establish our ears and eyes among the masses. From a military point of view, this was vital for the safeguard of national security and the establishments of an effective territorial control system, a major problem in counter-insurgency warfare.

But winning the sympathy of the people alone was not enough. The problem was how to motivate the masses to join in the fight against the Communists, directly or indirectly. This motivation challenge was both complex and difficult; it had been addressed by successive governments in South Vietnam.

The struggle on this front had many facets. The war was first and foremost an ideological conflict between Nationalists and Communists. To the people of South Vietnam, however, the Communists presented a nationalistic front: their cause was to fight for democracy, peace, and neutrality. They never mentioned communism or socialism; to their middle and high-level cadres, communist ideology was something taken for granted.

From the beginning of the conflict, the Nationalists had felt that need for an ideology of their own to light their path and serve as a basis for all of their programs. To meet this need and provide a doctrinal basis for the regime, the First Republic propounded the Personalist doctrine as an antidote to communism.

According to Mr. Ngo Dinh Nhu who developed this doctrine, Personalism was a blend of Western and Eastern philosophies designed for the total development of the individual in Vietnam's communal-type democracy. Personalism fostered the development of the individual, morally, spiritually, and physically in harmony with social needs of the community and as a step towards building the nation's political life. Each individual was to cultivate himself as a contribution to building society as a whole. Human rights and human dignity derived from hard work, and it was through work that democracy and freedom would be achieved. The advocates of personalism hoped to build a balanced democracy in which law and order would reign; they rejected both the excessive libertarianism of western bourgeois democracies and the restrictions and deceit of Communism.

After the fall of the First Republic and with it, the demise of personalism, subsequent nationalist governments advanced no other doctrines. In general, they espoused an uncompromising anti-Communist stance embedded in a vague nationalistic ideal. This ideal was to build a free and democratic society as opposed to human enslavement and regimentation under the control of international Communism.

To inculcate this ideal on the people, the GVN used all information media such as radio, TV, the performing arts, the press, posters and banners, announcements, notices, directives, and study groups. Depending on the requirements of each period, certain topics of information received the most comprehensive media coverage.

Two original forms of publicizing our ideal and neutralizing enemy propaganda were the Communist Denunciation Campaign and the study program. The Communist Denunciation Campaign followed immediately in the wake of the refugee exodus from North Vietnam. Understandably, it was emphasized for two years, until the end of 1956, and then was made a permanent study program. During that period, denouncing Communism took place throughout South Vietnam, in villages, hamlets, schools, government offices, military units, or private groups. In each meeting a speaker would present facts about the Communist doctrine and the subterfuges and crimes of the Communists. Sometimes a Communist defector was used to denounce Communist atrocities. As a result of this campaign in which the people actively tracked down underground Communist cadres, a large number of these cadres were arrested, and many documents, weapons and military supplies kept in caches were seized. In larger urban centers such as Saigon or provincial capitals, frequent anti-Communist mass rallies were held. In Saigon, for example, the Communist denunciation rally of February 1956 was attended by hundreds of thousands. In these rallies, speeches denouncing the Communists were frequently followed by confessions of Communist defectors, who expressed their penitence, burned the Communist flag, and took the oath of allegiance to the Nationalist government. These simplistic denunciations of

Communism probably had little effect on the intelligentsia, but from all indications, their impact on the popular masses was significant.

After 1957, the Anti-Communist Denunciation Campaign gave way to the Study Campaign. Radio broadcasts disseminated the logic and position of the government, and information teams carried the contents of these broadcasts into villages with public address systems. Every government office or military unit organized its own study sessions using materials prepared by the Ministry of Information or by the Psychological Warfare Directorate. In each session there was a lecture followed by discussion and a period devoted to questions and answers. The results of these periodic study sessions depended on the ability of the speaker as well as on the interest level of the topic. When they were established as routine, however, study sessions became boring and less frequently held, especially under the Second Republic. In many instances, performing art programs were introduced at study meetings to attract audiences; frequently the entertainment lasted much longer than the study session.

The information process designed to disseminate information for each administration went a step further by controlling and shutting out ideas and printed materials deemed detrimental to the official anti-Communist posture. For that reason every nationalist government endeavored, by one way or another to control the press and printed matter, which, to Western democracies, was a violation of the freedom of thought. But faced with an enemy who was a master of propaganda and deceit, the GVN seemed to have no choice since a straightforward implementation of the freedom of the press would amount to yielding an important advantage to the enemy. Communist propaganda agents would then easily infiltrate the free press and influence our writers who were usually impatient with restraints. Therefore, the requirements of the anti-Communist fight and the freedom of thought and of the press had to be weighed against each other in the context of South Vietnam.

Mobilizing the people also involved the regime's keen competition for stature with the masses. Although propounding the nationalist ideal contributed something to the cause of the regime, it was far more important to decry the prestige that the Communists were enjoying with large segments of the population because of their leadership role in the resistance against the French. For all its success, the campaign to denounce Communism and study its crimes was certainly not sufficient to confer a measure of legitimacy to the South Vietnamese regime.

To achieve this legitimacy, the First Republic took several actions. First, the feudalistic armed religious sects had to be put down. Then ex-Emperor Bao Dai had to be deposed as the symbol of a French-controlled puppet regime. But as long as the French High Commissioner and the French Expeditionary corps were present, the South Vietnamese people could not feel that the regime had changed. It was necessary therefore to remove the French presence to show that the regime was truly independent. Once the French had been expelled, the South Vietnamese government had also to prove that it was not overly influenced by U.S. advisors. Otherwise, the people would think that it was only a change of masters because the Communists never ceased to denounce our successive governments as American puppets. Though silent and passive, most Vietnamese people in the rural areas were extremely sensitive; from years of suffering under foreign domination they were naturally determined not to be slaves to foreigners. This was an important psychological fact to be heeded by any viable regime in Vietnam.

The competition for stature was epitomized in the persons of the leaders themselves. Centuries of monarchical rule and Confucian tradition conditioned Vietnamese to believe that patriotism was personal loyalty to the emperor. With that kind of mentality, a president of the new republic was not much different from an emperor of former times. Since partitioned Vietnam had two presidents, it was a matter of course that competition for the people's allegiance was strong between them. Ho Chi Minh had been deified by both the Communist and several Western scholars. Ngo Dinh Diem of South Vietnam, too, emerged as a leader of equal stature, perhaps Ho's most respected opponent. Propaganda had made both leaders appear to have a good origin, high achievements, talent, and moral excellence. So, if Ho Chi Minh's portrait was hung everywhere in Communist-controlled areas, Ngo Dinh Diem's pictures, too, had to be present in every home and government office in Nationalist-controlled areas. Despite his isolation, President Diem was revered by the rural people. After his assassination, no other South Vietnamese leader was ever again to enjoy the same prestige. For its part, North Vietnam continued to cling to "Uncle Ho's" image and, after his death, to his testament.

International standing was also part of national prestige. During the difficult and initial period when it had to place its house in order, the First Republic had been slow in cultivating foreign relations. It was not until 1958 that President Diem set about to win international sympathy and support. His success could be attributed to the immense prestige he enjoyed at home. South Vietnam quickly established relations with other nations of Asia and Africa. Then the Indian President and the Malaysian Prime Minister paid visits to Saigon. In contrast the Second Republic did not accomplish much in the area of foreign relations; its leader suffered from low popular esteem as a result.

Next there was the need to display national vitality, the ability to survive, and real strength. For North Vietnam, which had defeated the French and signed the Geneva Agreements, which called for reunification through general elections in two years, there was perhaps no need to prove its strength although this strength was constantly publicized. In addition North Vietnamese propaganda never failed to boast about the assistance and support that it received from the Communist "brother" countries. For South Vietnam which had nothing to its credit, the need to prove its strength was much more pressing. This strength should be demonstrated through the ability to survive, which the people had not fully perceived. It was necessary, therefore, to bring unity to nationalist forces and to reorganize and develop the armed forces. It was necessary to launch military operations, promote the pacification effort, set up military installations, and pioneer new lands as signs of permanent presence and settlement. Ceremonies and military parades conducted with a great deal of fanfare were also useful from the psychological point of view.

Showing off U.S. support, however, was a more delicate affair. President Diem's administration took great pains keeping this support in low profile so that it would not diminish national prestige in the eyes of the people. The Second Republic, with far less prestige, never hesitated to play up American support, perhaps to compensate for the lack of personal stature of its leaders.

Another form of competition for popular support, which also proved the most effective, was the devotion to serve the people. In this regard the GVN sometimes seemed to go out of its way, because in South Vietnam winning the support of the people meant the survival not only of the government but of the country as well. Competition with the North demanded that every South Vietnamese government from 1954 to 1975 did its best to insure a standard of living for its people higher than that enjoyed by the North. Owing to U.S. aid and a larger cultivated area, the South always far out distanced the North in this regard.

The rivalry in this area was translated into efforts of national development. Economic plans to include the building of an economic infrastructure were studied and implemented. During the First Republic, no sooner had the refugees been resettled than an effort was made to restore agricultural production to the pre-war level concurrently with plans to set up an industrial base. The Second Republic, which enjoyed greatly expanded American aid and the influx of allied troops, witnessed the extensive construction of roads, bridges, airports, and seaports, both new and renovated, and a modern telecommunications system. During this period towns and cities exhibited an appearance of affluence due primarily to a totally free import program. But this affluence was achieved at the expense of domestic industries.

In the efforts to better serve the people perhaps the key problem was to forge a corps of devoted civil servants and cadres and a military force that was friendly to the people. This was vital because the masses at the rice-roots level often judged their government through daily contacts with low-level, local officials. The First Republic had the advantage of a relatively secure situation which facilitated the conduct of normal governmental business. However, intensive war made it much more difficult for the Second Republic. President Diem also had the additional advantage of controlling a vast network of informers through the National Revolutionary movement, the Republican Youth, and especially the Can Lao Party. That tight control of local governments inspired respect for law, order and discipline and prevented the straying of officials at all levels. After his rule, though government officials knew they should serve the people whole-heartedly, there was much less incentive to resist temptations, especially in the face of a rising cost of living. If there were some relatively bright periods, they were due more to the security situation, the balance of forces, an active pacification program, and the productivity of the rural areas than to the accomplishments of our civil servants.

The behavior of RVNAF soldiers in military operations or in bivouacs near or in populated areas was extremely important. But the GVN never seemed able to train its soldiers properly in proselyting tactics; only a few well-led units could maintain good discipline. Under the First Republic there was tighter control in the field. During later periods, when the war had escalated and the armed forces greatly expanded, small unit commanders in general were lax in maintaining discipline. As a result the people really feared military operations. This was a serious weakness which was never satisfactorily corrected over the years.

Because the great majority of South Vietnamese lived in rural areas, rural policies were extremely important. For several years the Communists had raised the countryside to the level of a "key strategic area," and waged a kind of insurgency warfare whose strategy was to "use the countryside to surround and isolate the cities." They employed every technique to gain control gradually over the countryside, turning many places into areas of endless contest.

Under the First Republic an effort was made to reorganize village administration in order to achieve direct government control through province chiefs. Although this policy ran counter to tradition, it met with no resistance. After long years of war peasants returned to their home villages to work their land, and production rapidly rose. Economic recovery slowly but effectively moved ahead. The government also selected large areas in the hinterland for development and built roads and canals. In 1959, when the security situation was becoming more difficult, President Diem responded by launching the Agroville program designed to bring to the rural areas security and some comforts of city life. The program had just been initiated when guerrilla war broke out. The First Republic responded with the Strategic Hamlet program designed to maintain control and consolidate the vital rural areas.

During the Second Republic rural development was elevated to a national strategy. Peasants received assistance and care. Wherever security was established there appeared schools, dispensaries, information halls, and tractors. Agricultural extension programs such as the utilization of new seeds and fertilizers, improvement of animal husbandry methods brought new prosperity to the peasants.

Of prime importance in the rural policy was the land reform program. This reform was desirable since approximately two-thirds of the peasants in the Mekong Delta had no land to work. During the resistance war most landowners had left for the cities; now that peace had come they returned to reclaim their land and collect rents. With landowners determined to repossess their lands, the problem threatened to degenerate into a grave social conflict if the government did not intervene and resolve the problem.

The First Republic adopted a middle-of-the-road solution. Landowners with more than 100 hectares of farmland were forced to dispose of it. Tenants were allowed to purchase that land at a low cost and to relay it over a period of six years. Hesitant and limited, this land reform program was not very successful.

Under the Second Republic the land reform program was pursued more vigorously, and on a much larger scale. The "Land to The Tiller" program, implemented in 1970, was an instant success because of U.S. financial assistance. Termed revolutionary even by socialist standards, this program was probably the greatest success of the Nguyen Van Thieu government. With improved security the land reform program of 1970 brought about a new life to South Vietnam's countryside.

The South Vietnamese countryside also included the vast highlands with mountains and jungles which the Communists used as stepping stones to invade South Vietnam. Living scattered in this area were over 30 ethnic Montagnard tribes. President Diem personally devoted considerable attention to the highlands, which he often visited. He had contact with the hill tribes and promised them government assistance. Ethnic schools were opened in which tribal languages were taught in addition to Vietnamese. The First Republic also exploited forest resources and set up land development areas in the highlands. But the influx of Vietnamese lowlanders did not please the Montagnards very much. After a brief disorder caused by the FULRO, a rebellious Montagnard organization in 1964-65, the Second Republic treated the Montagnards with greater generosity. A new cabinet-level agency, the Ministry of Ethnic Development, was created to handle ethnic affairs. Montagnard military personnel and civil servants received greater consideration for appointment and promotion. Still, primarily because of Communist influence-buying propaganda, the ethnic problem was never completely solved.

Another technique of mobilizing the people was selecting the proper form of organization for the population. The enemy initiated several organizations, both overt and covert, to regiment the people. The GVN also placed great emphasis on this problem with the objective of rallying popular support for the war effort.

As early as 1955 the Ngo Dinh Diem government had embarked on popular mobilization through the National Revolutionary Movement. This movement quickly spread over the entire nation; it was a popular organization with local chapters at all levels. In provincial capitals and cities, there were chapters for every block, ward, quarter, and school district. These organizations took part in study sessions and held anti-Communist denunciation or other mass rallies directed by the government. In the civil service there was the League of National Revolutionary Civil Servants which, through its upperhanded operations, involved every government employee in study sessions and drastically changed the traditional apathy to which civil servants had been accustomed under French rule. This large-scale mobilization of the masses eventually gave the government the capability of massing popular support for other important tasks.

About 1959, led by Mme Ngo Dinh Nhu, the women's group within the National Revolutionary Movement grew into a new organization called the Women's Solidarity Movement. This organization played a leading role in charity work and visits to military installations, roles that were later taken over by the Young Republican Women's Association.

After several years of interruption similar popular organizations were revived under the Rural Development program in 1966. Rural Development Cadre teams, which were essentially improved versions of the Civil Action teams under the First Republic, took charge of developing various types of groups. These included organizations for women, senior citizens, boys and girls, and self-defense teams.

In a war situation, however, popular mobilization was successful only if the people could be motivated to take an active part in the defense of their homes and neighborhoods. On the pattern of the self-defense organization or people's militia of 1945-54 the First Republic had initially established village defense groups. By the time strategic hamlets came into being these village defense groups had grown in size and became known as Young Republican Men. Distinguished by the mechanic's blue uniform of its members, the Young Republican Men's organization had offices in all towns and cities and were placed under the overall command of Mr. Ngo Dinh Nhu. By 1963 the membership of this organization totaled over one million who had received military training and part of whom had been armed. Besides the Young Republican Men, there were the Young Republican Women and groups of civil servants who had undergone paramilitary training and were armed and given guard duty at government offices.

During 1964-65 the Nguyen Khanh government organized the Fighting Youth in villages and Civil Defense teams in towns and cities. While Fighting Youth members were armed for self-defense in rural areas, the Civil Defense was essentially an organization of civil servants and urban dwellers who took action only in case of disorder or disaster.

Under the Second Republic, especially after the 1968 Tet Offensive, self-defense forces went through a period of great expansion and became known as People's Self-Defense Forces (PSDF). In many places local people volunteered for duty and requested weapons to defend themselves against the Communists. By 1970 the PSDF included four million members, of which one million were combatants equipped with 400,000 individual weapons. This was a considerable force. In many areas PSDF members had fought gallantly and sustained casualties under enemy attack.

Finally, apart from the effort to mobilize the masses as a political power base, a fighting force, and as an effective way to undermine the enemy's strength, nationalist governments under the First and Second Republic also attempted to set up a government's party. Mr. Ngo Dinh Nhu, President Diem's political advisor, had founded the Can Lao Nhan Vi Party which was destined to play the vanguard role of national revolution.

The Can Lao Party began to grow as soon as Mr. Diem assumed powers in 1954; its membership was recruited discreetly. The Party never operated overtly, had no official headquarters, and held no rallies. It seemed as if the Can Lao Party had served only as the eyes and ears of the leaders in power; therefore, it never had the official status of a political party. Under the Second Republic President Nguyen Van Thieu founded the Democratic Party in 1971. The Party was hastily put together by a massive recruitment effort, carried out primarily by some cabinet ministers and province chiefs. The Party made its first public appearance in Saigon and operated as the party of the government in power. But the low standing of the government, the opposition of other nationalist parties, and popular apathy had an adverse impact on the status of the Democratic Party.

Motivating the people to join the fight against the Communists was an absolute requirement but it was difficult to achieve. To be successful the regime had to be trusted by the people. It should have a just cause, prestige, and attractive qualities. It should also be able to convince the people, through its achievements, that it was worthy of their sacrifices.

President Diem had personal prestige and moral rectitude, the qualities of a good leader. He had devoted all of his efforts to build the nation and motivate the people. Some of his collaborators, however, had committed errors that plunged the nation into chaos and led to the collapse of the regime. Suffering from a lack of prestige and unable to solve internal problems and mobilize the masses to join in the anti-Communist struggle, subsequent governments came to depend heavily on the United States. The advent of U.S. participation in the war brought about far-reaching consequences which affected the entire fabric of South Vietnamese society.

CHAPTER III

American Influence on South Vietnamese Society

Significant Contrasts

The Indochinese conflict brought together the Republic of Vietnam and the United States. Although this marriage of convenience was dictated by a common purpose -- to contain Communist expansion and especially North Vietnam's attempt to annex the South -- the alliance brought to the surface certain basic incompabilities between the two nations. As Kipling had observed, "West is West, and East is East, and the twain shall never meet," it was inevitable that differences could be expected. Vietnam and the U.S. were so dissimilar in origins, background, civilization, and environment that they stood at the very antipodes of the human spectrum. Such differences could only be mitigated or ignored but never totally nullified. In former times the Chinese had devoted many years to come to sociable terms with Vietnam, yet they never succeeded in reconciling all the differences. It was obvious that time was the essential ingredient to bring about mutual understanding and a harmonious working relationship.

In 1954 South Vietnamse had only a sketchy knowledge but generally favorable opinion of the United States. In the eyes of South Vietnamese at that time the United States was like a magic rope to cling to in order to escape from the extremely dangerous quicksand in which they had found themselves. Most educated urban Vietnamese saw the United States as the epitome of democracy, the most affluent and modern nation on earth, a world power without colonial ambitions and whose assistance to other nations under the Marshall Plan was universally applauded, and finally as a staunchly anti-Communist friend that bore the major brunt in the Korean conflict during 1950-1953. To rural South Vietnamese, however, the United States was a total stranger. Later when the United States entered the war some rural people regarded it, through the refracting prism of Communist propaganda, as an aggressor. However, most submitted to the urban view that the Americans had come as friends.

In addition to this very general perception of the United States, very few Vietnamese had a chance to know Americans as individuals. Initially, therefore, Vietnamese who had to deal with Americans made use of their experience with the French in maintaining a relationship. For their part, except for those who had some connection with the Vietnam war, the majority of the American people probably knew little about Vietnam. Those who did acquired their knowledge mostly from books on Vietnam written by French and American authors. The advantage conferred by this knowledge was that the general information on the Vietnamese people and their ways and customs helped the Americans to overcome the awkwardness they might have felt in their first contacts with the Vietnamese. But there was a disadvantage in that the superficial or biased observations of Western, especially French, writers had seemed to perpetuate a body of erroneous preconceived ideas about the Vietnamese people and Vietnamese society.

Most Americans came to Vietnam on a one-year tour of duty. Others, who had extended or additional tours, seldom paid attention to the true character of the people with whom they had contact and of the society among which they lived; with a few exceptions and because of their assignments or duties, they rarely concerned themselves with the inherent differences between the two peoples.

A fundamental and most important difference between the two partners during the war was in the concept of time and action. While Americans regarded action as a compulsion and something to be performed aggressively in the shortest possible time, Vietnamese seemed to view time as an eternal commodity, an ingredient of the panacea to all problems. For this reason, inaction in the immediate present might be a form of action and was acceptable; it did not mean laziness, evasion, or passivity, but merely implied waiting for an opportune moment to act.

Vietnamese differed from Americans in the way they solved a problem. While the Americans often arrived at an optimum solution, the Vietnamese usually preferred a multiple approach. This inclination was a trait of the Vietnamese character which probably originated from Buddhist and Confucian influence. Buddha taught us that there is not just one buddha -- the Enlightened One -- but anyone following the right path can work toward his own enlightenment as a buddha. Confucius taught us to use the golden mean in our daily life. According to him things are never slanted to one side and are subject to change by the natural order. Thus, the right attitude to adopt is toward the middle of every issue. The experience of Vietnam with its numerous vicissitudes, its changes of dynasties, its political misfortunes of the 19th and 20th centuries had probably reinforced among Vietnamese the predilection for a multiple approach to solving problems. This occasionally caused unwitting Americans, especially American advisors, to criticize their Vietnamese counterparts for their indecisiveness, their lack of dynamism and drive.

Family attachment of the Vietnamese was known to Americans, but this loyalty as well as the extended family obligations were sometimes beyond American comprehension. Vietnamese society had always been a restricted community. The nuclear family always lay within the limits of the extended family. When members of the extended family got married, loyalty to the extended family was further expanded to encompass the new nuclear families. Thus it was that in human relations feelings normally took precedence over reason among Vietnamese, and though many Vietnamese realized this as being a weakness it was not easily overcome. Unlike Americans, Vietnamese gave little heed to social organizations and seldom regarded social activities as part of the individual's life, the exception being North Vietnamese Communists. No political parties in South Vietnam could be ranked among U.S. parties in terms of the role they played in the lives of their members. The relation between the people and the national leader in Vietnam was also different from what it is in the United States. While Americans make a distinction between the person of the President and his office, Vietnamese tended to regard the two as being inseparable. Such an attitude must have begun in feudal times, when "being loyal to the king is being loyal to the country," and was fostered by every South Vietnamese leader. These leaders identified themselves with the regimes they were leading so that loyalty to the person of the leader was the only way to be loyal to the political establishment.

The disastrous offshoot of this attitude was that anyone who made positive contributions to the system, the government, or the head of an official organization, was regarded as a loyalist, and anyone who did not cooperate was regarded as a member of the opposition.

Another difference between Vietnamese and Americans was perhaps most significant since it concerned the general attitude toward the war. With the war lasting almost continuously since 1946 most Vietnamese, though considering it a scourge, had come to regard it as part of their lives. Many considered peace and the end of all hostilities as wishful thinking and thus reconciled themselves to living with it. This attitude led many Americans to criticize Vietnamese for negativism, flinching resolve, and defeatism.

Important as these differences were, not all Americans fully recognized them, which resulted in misunderstanding and lost opportunities to bridge the gap when cooperation was at stake.

Major Objectives and their Impact

Throughout its association with Vietnam, the United States had three primary objectives: to assist South Vietnam in building adequate strength to resist aggression by North Vietnam, to help South Vietnam build a democratic state and, to help South Vietnam develop its economy. Each of these major areas of interest had an impact on South Vietnamese society.

These objectives were indicated by President Eisenhower when he wrote to Mr. Ngo Dinh Diem in 1954: "The purpose of this offer is to assist the government of South Vietnam in developing and maintaining a strong viable state, capable of resisting attempted subversion or aggression through military means."[1]

The military might of U.S. forces was the subject of great admiration among South Vietnamese when the United States was victorious at the end of World War II and subsequently fought Red China and North Korea to a standstill during the Korean War. Providing military aid to South Vietnam in 1954, the United States was using its war experience in helping reorganize the Republic of Vietnam Armed Forces. The United States then advocated building a regular army of about 120,000 men capable of resisting North Vietnam's aggressive designs which were presumed to materialize under the form of an invasion. Carrying over the strategic thinking developed during the Korean conflict, the United States envisioned the RVNAF as just having limited resistance capability. In case of invasion, their role was to fight a delaying action pending the intervention of SEATO forces. However, this position on the total size and requirements of our armed forces was destined to change drastically as Communist objectives and plans were surfaced.

The commitment of U.S. forces into the war in 1965 provided South Vietnamese civilian and military leaders with new hope. American modern equipment, superior firepower, and scientific and technological knowledge as applied to the war effort nurtured South Vietnam's expectations for a strong military machine similar to that of the United States at some future time. The excellent staff work, organization, and operation of U.S. forces, as exemplified in staff briefings replete with carefully researched data and captivating presentation techniques, had never failed to fascinate Vietnamese military leaders.

The tendency to pattern the RVNAF organization and tactics after the U.S. model was reinforced in combat operations in which Vietnamese forces, whether operating separately or in concert with U.S. forces,

---

[1] Department of State Bulletin Nov. 15, 1954, pp. 735-736.

gradually acquired the habits of a rich man's army, giving weight to materiel and firepower and substituting firepower for manpower. This imitation of U.S. organization and operation involved a number of important problems which hardly anyone noticed at the time. Being a nation with immense resources, the United States could afford a modern and expensive defense establishment. But the small and impoverished RVN and its society could maintain a strong military force and fight the war along U.S. lines only with prolonged American aid. Furthermore, while being obsessed with modeling themselves after the U.S. forces and employing U.S. military doctrine and tactics, the RVNAF were unwittingly neglecting their own experience in counter-insurgency warfare, their anti-guerrilla techniques, and their knowledge of the enemy, which were the advantages accruing only to an indigenous army and which U.S. conventional forces could not have enjoyed to the same degree.

This United States objective of helping the RVN develop adequate strength to resist aggression gradually influenced several changes at all echelons in our society. As U.S. military presence phased out, RVNAF authorized strength reached over one million personnel. Almost every family had one or more of its immediate members in uniform often serving considerable distances from their homes for extended periods. This interference with our long established routine of daily life was felt by entire family groups.

This great expansion also produced many technicians and specialists to meet military requirements. However, as years evolved some were released from the Armed Forces because of wounds, age or other health problems. This category of personnel would usually seek employment in their areas of speciality resulting in more families moving into urban areas or locations where employment was available.

A most significant impact on South Vietnamese society, however, was the drain on our total manpower caused by the expansion of our armed forces. This had a direct effect on our communities, collective activities and interests, standards of living, conduct and organized patterns of normal life.

During the process of helping the RVN build adequate military strength, the massive military presence of the United States in South

Vietnam had a disadvantage in that it usually eclipsed the role of the RVNAF. The U.S. military presence naturally attracted the attention of the foreign and especially the U.S. press. Reports on the war were heavily documented in terms of U.S. performance and enemy activities. Conspicuously, most RVNAF activities were left out of news coverage, and when reported on a few occasions, the slant was invariably directed against their shortcomings or worse.

This pattern, which was repeated over and over again, was a constant irritation to RVNAF leaders and infused doubts in the minds of those military men who were suffering from a feeling of inadequacy. It even caused some people of South Vietnam to believe that the RVNAF were incapable of protecting them. As for the enemy, he stood to gain by the reports of the foreign press that unwittingly seemed to be extolling Communist exploits. This unfortunate condition contributed to the complete collapse of faith among RVNAF ranks and throughout our society in general at a time when U.S. aid and apparent interest was dwindling.

Assisting South Vietnam in developing a true democracy, the second objective of the United States, was emphasized in 1954 by Senator John F. Kennedy, "To assist a nation taking the first feeble step toward the complexity of a republican form of government."[2]

Building democracy in South Vietnam was therefore a national goal not only widely proclaimed by the GVN to the Vietnamese people but also publicized by the U.S. government for the American public. In time it became a yardstick that the U.S. applied in its assessment of and justification for aid to this country.

Although sharing the common desire and objective of making South Vietnam a democratic nation, the U.S. and the RVN governments did not always completely agree on how to proceed. The U.S. maintained that

---

[2] *American's Stake in Vietnam: Anatomy of a Conflict*, by Wesley R. Fishet, F.E. Peacock Publishers, Inc., 1968, p. 143.

the establishment of a republican form of government in South Vietnam with democratic institutions and the application of individual liberties should satisfy the aspirations of the South Vietnamese and help defeat Communism. Although concurring in principle, the GVN held that, in a country being threatened by Communist subversion, democracy could not mean a total implementation of all rights and freedoms in view of the political, security, and economic situation and of the level of education of the people. To the GVN, unrestrained implementation of all freedoms would lead to an uncontrollable situation which allowed Communist elements to operate more easily by taking advantage of opportunities in the democratic system. Regardless of the approach and time required for the process leading to a true democracy, it was obvious that it would have an influence on our common traditions, institutions and eventually our society in general.

Unlike on the military front, where the GVN was almost totally aligned on the U.S. position, on the political scene the GVN always endeavored to maintain its own course when warranted by the situation. The first Constitution of the RVN, proclaimed on 26 October 1956, though patterned after the U.S. Constitution, gave broad powers to the President, which was a main feature of the French Constitution of 1946. The Constitution notwithstanding, the Diem administration did not always seem to respect it in practice. A case in point was the failure of the government to activate the Council for the Upholding of the Constitution and the Economic Council, both of which were provided for by the Constitution but were not established until six years later in spite of American pressure.

Free elections are typical of all democracies. For South Vietnam, elections had the added meaning of providing a yardstick to compare its democratic form of government with the totalitarian regime of North Vietnam, where the National Assembly, elected in 1946, was not reelected until 14 years later. The South was indeed making greater strides in holding periodic congressional and presidential elections. However, the Diem government did not want elections at the rice-roots level. A 1956 law provided for the appointment of village councils by province chiefs upon recommendation by district chiefs and approval by the Ministry of the Interior.

One major difference between the First and the Second Republic was the extent to which the GVN yielded to American influence. The 1967 Constitution of the Second Republic no doubt bore greater affinity with the U.S. Constitution than the 1956 Constitution in that it instituted a bicameral national legislature and the Supreme Court. Village elections were also initiated in April 1967; to the United States this was a sign of progress toward true democracy.

To the majority of South Vietnamese, however, elections were not necessarily a sign of true democracy or a way to meet the wishes of the people. The South Vietnamese people, especially those in the rural areas, were in general either unfamiliar with elections or unable to grasp their meaning. They did not believe that elections would result in a better life for them, or that those elected would work for their advancement. Among urban dwellers and opposition parties there was also little faith in elections because they always suspected the government of committing fraud. They, too, did not seem to trust those elected to fight for the rights of the people. To the discontented, therefore, elections were often an opportunity to vent their frustration and opposition to the government by casting their ballots for whoever opposed the government. Hence, elections did not always serve the national cause or accurately reflect the true wishes of the people.

During our evolution toward a true democracy the coup d'etat became a popular tool of power groups. Coups become such a fearful obsession for all South Vietnamese leaders that their main effort was to prevent them by appointing close and loyal friends to sensitive posts such as the CMD, major units, military regions and armed services. Every other consideration seemed to be subordinated to this concern. The net result was a reduction in the performance level of the RVNAF since many of our major activities and units were riddled with factionalism, suspicion, and infighting and the fact that military leaders were contending for power by engaging in politics.

Since a coup was never a substitute for real authority and because popular allegiance still had to be won, the leader had to secure supporters from his own faction and insure his own protection by placing trusted people and relatives in all key positions. Consequently, what bound these people together were primarily material incentives and shared power, not just devotion to a just cause or ideology or the welfare of South Vietnamese society.

In its third area of major interest, helping South Vietnamese develop economically, the United States without question had a direct influence on our society. This was reflected at every level from the activities of our highest institutions down to our hamlets and villages.

The U.S. and RVN agreed that a strong, viable economy was the very foundation upon which a developing nation must base its future in all other endeavors, socially, politically and militarily. For this reason the United States, at much expense to its taxpayers, applied considerable effort in helping the RVN with our economic problems; the common objective was to build a strong and independent Vietnam.

Major programs were initiated with sound objectives in vast and complex areas such as agriculture, public affairs, public health, public services and the training of a skilled labor force. This emphasis on skilled labor concurrent with the expansion of the RVNAF during Vietnamization resulted in the additional use of women, plus the old and young of both sexes. These initiatives, especially in a country long engaged in war, changed our normal standards of living, influenced our daily lives and even contributed to the separation of family members. Concurrently, as Western imports, previously considered luxury items, became available our society became more materialistic.

The fact that the value of the Vietnamese piaster was pegged to that of the American dollar had enormous consequences for South Vietnam's economy. Under the First Republic, Vietnamese authorities refused to devalue the paister as advised by the United States. Although this devaluation was meant to reestablish parity between the two currencies, its implementation would have had a profound psychological impact on the masses and was adamantly opposed by President Diem. Finally, the piaster's exchange value was allowed to float freely in relation to the U.S. dollar under the Second Republic. Additionally, no South Vietnamese government was ever able to combat the thriving black market for the U.S. dollar, a situation that totally destabilized the piaster. And runaway inflation came along which resulted in endless spirals of price hikes.

In addition to the impacts that U.S. objectives exerted on South Vietnam militarily, politically, and economically, there was the significant imprint that U.S. aid and the U.S. presence left on South Vietnamese social life. As was true with the usual effect of Western civilization on traditional oriental life, this imprint had its good and bad marks, and both combined to change South Vietnamese society.

Social Impact of the American Presence

South Vietnamese might have differed on how and to what extent the presence of over one half of a million U.S. troops and advisers had influenced South Vietnamese society. Most agreed, however, that this presence affected primarily the urban segment and had a lesser effect on the rural people. They also agreed that the American influence was perhaps more pervasive than had been thought because among the many impacts it had created there were tangible ones in the areas of military, political, and economic endeavor as well as intangible ones, such as in cultural and social behavior.

No one could perhaps deny that the American presence was a psychological boost to South Vietnamese morale. All appeared to be convinced that as long as U.S. personnel were involved the U.S. was not about to abandon South Vietnam. South Vietnamese nationalists also felt grateful for the substantial aid and military intervention of the U.S. At the very least, this aid and intervention had saved South Vietnam from probable collapse in 1965 and helped it turn around the outcome of the war in 1968 and 1972. All this had made it possible for South Vietnam to survive until 1975.

Despite the ravages of the war, the urban society of South Vietnam seemed to thrive in prosperity. The majority of urban and certain wealthy rural people enjoyed all the amenities of modern life:

automobiles, motorcycles, air conditioners, refrigerators, television, radio, etc., which were available on a large scale only to industrially-developed Asian countries such as Japan. Most remarkably, even the ordinary working class was often able to share in what had usually been restricted to wealthy elements of society. Most urban and suburban households owned a radio receiver, and one out of ten a television set. Private transportation means such as motorcycles and bicycles were usually available for every working family, including some living in rural areas. Electricity, once confined to big cities, gradually expanded to all district towns and most of the suburbs surrounding major cities. Had it not been for enemy sabotage and war destructiveness, rural electrification could have been a reality during the 60's.

The presence of U.S. troops brought about a marked improvement in land communications. Roads were enlarged, extended, or newly built along with the rehabilitation of old bridges and the construction of new ones. This improved and extended road system not only facilitated inter-regional and interprovincial communication; it also brought the cities closer to the countryside and narrowed the urban-rural social gap. In addition to convenient roads and an expanded domestic air service, the most significant improvement in waterway communication was the availability of motorboats. This was particularly important for the rural people of the Mekong Delta whose living depended on the crisscrossing system of rivers and canals. If in some localities the rural farmers could not purchase motorboats for their convenient use, it was not because of financial limitations but because of security reasons. In these areas motorboats were considered a military utility, and their purchases were curtailed.

Except for those farmlands that were left uncultivated because of war and insecurity, most areas under cultivation benefited from farm mechanization and modern farming techniques. Tilling machines, chemical fertilizers, and insecticides, which were imported with U.S. aid money, made it possible for the farmers to increase crop production significantly. The average yield of rice per hectare rose remarkably owing to the import of new hybrid seeds whose use was greatly encouraged. Chicken raising in particular had become a new expanding industry which quickly gained in popularity with the import of U.S. breeds, U.S. feed, and U.S. techniques. More importantly the 1970 agrarian reform program, which was perhaps the most tangible tribute to U.S. economic and technological aid, had brought about some true measure of social equality and might someday change South Vietnam's social fabric entirely.

In public health, there was no doubt that U.S.-sponsored MEDCAP activities had resulted in better health care for those areas where indigenous doctors were a rarity. In addition, district and village health stations and the availability of U.S.-provided medicine for most medical treatment needs also contributed to better health for the rural peasantry. Several diseases heretofore considered fatal such as lung tuberculosis had been brought under control and were no longer incurable. This was possible due to the highly-specialized and advanced U.S. treatment methods which were a far cry from the French general practice approach. For this reason, a certain number of hospitals and dispensaries established by the U.S. in South Vietnam quickly became popular among local patients because of their effectiveness.

In education, school facilities had expanded manyfold over the years in keeping with educational development trends. Aside from higher education institutes in major cities, high and elementary schools were available in all district towns and villages which brought education to within reach of the rural child. Education was further advanced by the support of U.S. funds which provided better school books and other supplies for the needy students. English also became the major foreign language option for most students who preferred it to French for obvious reasons. English schools, both U.S.-sponsored and private, mushroomed in every major city which catered to increasing numbers of adults, among them civil servants, servicemen, and people who had business connections with Americans. The traditional culture of Vietnam with its waning Chinese and French heritage, was now enriched by the new impact of American language and culture.

While middle-aged South Vietnamese naturally tended to be conservative and adhered with nostalgia to traditional Vietnamese and French culture, the young people found American culture fashionable and quickly adapted themselves to it. This was evident in the way they dressed and the kind of music they adored. In many urban homes, people used lively, bold colors for the interior, an obvious imitation of American decoration style. More conspicuously, the tall and stylish buildings which were rapidly constructed during the 1965-70 period for the purpose of leasing to Americans added a modern outlook to major cities making them more beautiful and impressive. With the buildup of U.S. troops, apartment buildings also began to develop and expand rapidly. This was quite a change in living pattern for many South Vietnamese who had been familiar only with single family dwellings or extended family cohabitation within the same house.

As a result of the American buildup, a great number of people turned to activities directly or indirectly connected with services for U.S. units and troops. These were contractors, entrepreneurs, businessmen, and some civilian employees serving in U.S. organizations. Because of lucrative service contracts and business dealings, these people gained sizeable incomes, and many rapidly amassed great fortunes. High income and quick wealth also turned these people into a new privileged urban class, a class by itself that never existed in Vietnamese society before.

Another emerging social element was the prostitutes and bar girls whose numbers quickly multiplied with the buildup of U.S. troops. Socially considered the basest and most contemptible, these elements seemed to take to the good material life with a revenge. With the good and easy money they made, they spent it in far-out fashions and a flashy, abandoned life style which exerted a bad influence on women and led many among them, the gullible and the morally loose, to follow in their sinful steps. This unwittingly upset the usually puritan mores of traditional South Vietnamese society.

The next privileged social group consisted of civilian employees serving in U.S. organizations whose salaries were two or three times larger than those of GVN civil servants or servicemen. This disparity in income coupled with a most lopsided distribution of wealth was a major source of frustration and social injustice. The civil servants, servicemen, and policemen, those who received fixed and much lower salaries, considered themselves and were in fact the most underprivileged elements of society. They were understandably frustrated because the compensation they were receiving did not measure up to the sacrifices and contributions they made for the sake of the country's survival. By contrast, the people who made the most money were those who practically contributed nothing to the war effort.

As a result of U.S. aid benefits and the free-flowing money spent by U.S. troops, the urban society of South Vietnam became more and more materialistic-oriented. Material wealth eventually became the yardstick by which human fulfillment was measured. As people attached more value to material acquisitions, morality suffered a great setback. This materialistic race involved the majority of urban people, including those so-called spiritual leaders and custodians of morality. It broke up families, fostered crimes, and fomented juvenile delinquency. The ills were so widespread that responsible civic leaders warned of social decadence but were impotent to do anything about it. New fads such as long hair, hippy living, and punk rock, unquestionably the expressions of an American subculture, caught on with an urban youth devoted to free love and fast living. Bars and night clubs which catered to the GI on leave were also the hangouts for the degenerate urban youth. Drugs such as marijuana and heroine, which were almost non-existent before the war, now became a thriving business for trafiquants and pushers who adhered to the American GI clientele. These drugs soon found their way into big cities and made victims among the youth of rich families. All of these happenings accentuated the contrast between the cities and the rural areas and made the rural peasant feel increasingly alienated from his urban brother. Gradually, it seemed that the South Vietnamese people were living in two separate worlds far removed from each other.

Despite these undesirable side-effects, both U.S. aid and the U.S. presence enabled South Vietnam to meet several serious challenges and survive after the U.S. pull-out. Accustomed to the U.S. presence, however, the South Vietnamese suddenly found the American absence a great void and big psychological shock. The withdrawal of U.S. military and civilian advisors from Vietnamese governmental and military structure created a vacuum, especially in the areas of research and planning and supporting resources. Ordinarily, if a corps/MR commander wanted to replace a province chief, he had to submit his recommendation through channels to the Prime Minister and the President for approval. Now if the U.S. corps/MR senior advisor was present and agreed with the corps/MR commander's recommendation, he would only need to talk to the Prime Minister or the President, and the province chief would be quickly removed. Such was the power enjoyed by U.S. senior advisors in South Vietnam. Politically, however, the absence of U.S. advisors was a blessing because it offered a good opportunity for South Vietnam to try harder, to gain self-confidence, and to prove that it had reached maturity in all areas of national endeavor. It also helped combat the pernicious effect of the Communist propaganda line that "South Vietnam was a puppet of American imperialism."

On balance, the net result of the American presence in South Vietnam was that no matter how well-intentioned and dedicated Americans had proved to be, the Vietnamese always felt that their friends were playing the leading role in all fields of endeavor. They also had the impression that the U.S. was behind everything that ever happened to South Vietnam. The inescapable feeling among some Vietnamese nationalists who gave their allegiance to the Republic of Vietnam was that the South could never have made its just cause prevail and used it effectively as a viable alternative to Communism. Hence, there were those who seriously questioned the usefulness of what they were doing and especially the wisdom of American participation in the war.

On its part, the United States itself must have perceived that the essential thing was for the South to have a worthy cause to fight for, and that its policy should have been conceived with that in mind. Yet in its haste to achieve quick success and a military victory the United States had been too eager to take everything upon itself and allowed itself to control almost every facet of the RVN's effort in the process. So encompassing and visible was this control that it left the RVN utterly passive, dependent, subservient, and unable to make decisions for its own sake and negated whatever cause the RVN had built for its struggle. This domination was plain to the people of South Vietnam, to the world, and to our enemy in the North as well. This was the inevitable consequence of American eagerness, competitiveness, and work ethics which are among distinctive features of the American people and society. If in the complex struggle against Communism in the South, these traits had been made to work in harmony with those of Vietnamese individual and social character, the results might have been different. And if the U.S. had been more aware of the nature of South Vietnamese society and its effect on the conduct of the war, then it could have devoted more efforts to help South Vietnam resolve or alleviate its social problems, a main impediment to success over the years.

CHAPTER IV

Social Problems

Discrimination and Factionalism

In the mid-16th century when Nguyen Hoang, a forefather of the Nguyen dynasty, petitioned Prince Trinh Kiem for the governorship of Thuan Hoa, the poor, troubled, and remotest land on the southern frontier, the idea of secession must have been his main and true motive.[1] As history was later to prove his vision true, he believed that "In the Hoanh Son (the Annamitic Cordillera) there must be security for thousands of generations." Knowing that his posture was too weak to fight the Trinh warlords after they had killed his eldest brother, Nguyen Hoang was planning his own escape and nurturing the dream of carving out his own kingdom in the far South. This was perhaps the earliest and most explanatory evidence of the traditional North-South rift in the history of Vietnam.

For the next 150 years, from the barren and lawless township of Thuan Hoa, the Nguyen warlords expanded the frontiers of Vietnam southward to the Mekong Delta after destroying the Champa Kingdom and annexing parts of Chenla (present-day Cambodia) in the process. The southern part of divided Vietnam had become then a haven for persons who had lost their standing in the North, the discontented intelligentsia, those who opposed the Trinh rule, and the venturesome poor in quest of a better living. Though sparsely populated and endowed with scant resources, the South under the Nguyen had successfully and repeatedly repelled violent attacks by the Trinh through the sheer force of their autarky spirit.

---

[1] Thuan Hoa in the old days is presently in the area of Hue City.

As Vietnamese territory grew in length, communication became difficult and the differences deepened between North and South. As in the old days, the imperial court could only maintain loose control over outlying areas. By force of protracted separation the traditions and customs originating in the Northern heartland became relaxed in the free and pioneer spirit of the frontier. Contact with, and borrowing from, Indian civilization through the intermediary of the Chams and Khmers also brought about significant alterations in the heavily Chinese-influenced culture of the North.

Time and isolation finally combined to accentuate these changes in the South. Though essentially the same language, Vietnamese underwent some modifications in its diffusion. In the area of the Perfume River, alteration came in the form of lower pitches and restricted pitch variations in the tonal contrast; in the Mekong Delta and the Dong Nai River basin, linguistic expression became plainer and more direct.[2] Over the length of Vietnam, not only did the accent change from one province to another, but the vocabulary and modes of expression also differed. The milder climate of the South seemed to favor the pioneers; they did not need heavy clothes as in the North, and their housing could be built less elaborately because of fewer typhoons. The immensity and fertility of the land and abundance of food also made life easier and had a distinctive effect on the character of the southern people. Because of fewer hardships and less competition there was no need for exertion and aggressiveness.

When the French occupied Vietnam in the middle of the 19th century, they strictly applied a policy of "rule by division." Vietnam was partitioned into three regions and each placed under a different administrative system. North Vietnam (Tonkin) and Central Vietnam (Annam)

---

[2] The Perfume River flows through the area of Hue. The Dong Nai and Mekong Rivers wind their courses east and west of Saigon, respectively.

became French "protectorates" which were nominally under the Nguyen emperor but ruled by French governors. South Vietnam (Cochinchina), being a colony, was governed directly by the French. The status of Vietnamese nationals differed from region to region, with Southerners being the most favored. Movement from one region to another was made difficult; in fact, traveling from North to South Vietnam was not unlike crossing the border into another country. The recruitment of Northern laborers to work on Southern plantations and their merciless exploitation by French operators eventually became a haunting memory among Northerners. Divisiness between regions therefore widened to the point of becoming alienation.

In 1946 while the Ho Chi Minh delegation was on its way to Fontainebleau, France to discuss the reunification and independence of Vietnam the French High Commissioner for Indochina, Admiral d'Argenlieu, proclaimed Cochinchina a separate republic (naturally under French protection). An autonomous all-South Vietnamese government was established and fomented by the French, the undercurrent of secession with and hostility toward North Vietnam came out into the open. In Saigon secessionists sought out Northern-born citizens and arrested, beat, or ostracized them. During this period Northerners living in the South had to conceal their identity and imitated the Southern accent to protect themselves. Even in 1949 when Bao Dai accepted to cooperate with the French, and a national government was established for all three regions, these feelings of hatred were not completely erased.

The Geneva Agreements, concluded on 20 July 1954, partitioned the country at the 17th parallel. A million Northerners, migrants and government employees (from the northern part of Central Vietnam) came to the South. Thus was the amalgam process begun. If this mixing came about as a blessing in that it entailed the integration of modes of thinking, ways of life, mores and customs of the three regions into a national culture, it also generated a great deal of friction and smoldering rivalries.

Refugees were given food, money, jobs, and land to resettle themselves by the Ngo Dinh Diem government. Refugee military officers and government employees enjoyed more trust because of their proven anti-

Communist position. But cadres from Central Vietnam were understandably the ones most trusted by President Diem. The overwhelming presence of Northern and Central officials in the administration and the military at this time caused a great deal of resentment among the Southern population. Refugees from North and Central Vietnam, who lived in resettlement areas and whom the local populace regarded as a privileged group, took years to integrate into the mainstream of South Vietnamese social life.

The Ngo Dinh Diem government must have tried hard to curb the effect of regional difference. Southern-born individuals of prominence were given good treatment and appointed to highly visible but ceremonial positions. For example Mr. Diem selected a high-level functionary under the French colonial government, Mr. Nguyen Ngoc Tho, as his Vice-President. Mr. Truong Vinh Le and his successor, Mr. Tran Van Lam, became President of the National Assembly, and Mr. Nguyen Van Vang was appointed Delegate of the Government; these were but a few examples. Mr. Diem also took great care in selecting most province chiefs of the Mekong Delta from among Southerners. Similar efforts were visible in the armed forces. Several Southern-born generals received important assignments at this time such as Generals Le Van Ty, Duong Van Minh, Tran Van Minh, Tran Van Don, Le Van Kim, Do Cao Tri, Mai Huu Xuan and Tran Tu Oai.

However, key power-wielding or sensitive positions were mostly entrusted to loyal Central Diemists. For example the III Corps, which defended the capital city of Saigon, was placed under the successive commands of General Le Van Nghiem and General Ton That Dinh. The Airborne troops and the Special Froces, whose strike units were on constant alert, were commanded by Colonel Nguyen Chanh Thi and Colonel Le Quang Tung respectively. The Military Security Service had Colonel Do Mau as its chief. The Armor command and infantry divisions located in vital areas were all placed under trusted Central-born officers. Other important government officials and the chiefs of key provinces were also appointed with similar considerations. It was thus difficult to defend the Ngo Dinh Diem government as being free of regionalism.

Regionalism under the First Republic was further compounded by religious discrimination. President Ngo Dinh Diem's family were devout

Catholics of long standing. His eldest living brother, Archbishop Ngo Dinh Thuc, was the senior prelate in South Vietnam. In the Confucian tradition the eldest brother had tremendous authority over his younger siblings. Father Thuc commanded substantial influence in the Vinh Long diocese, which saw significant developments during his tenure. Here was the seedbed of many a national program which highlighted the regime of the First Republic such as the Nhan Vi (Personalist) cadre training center, the Republican Youth, and the Strategic Hamlets. Catholic clerics had easy access to the Independence Palace, and this rapport naturally resulted in governmental favors to Catholic organizations.

If these favors had been confined to religious matters, perhaps they would not have incurred so much criticism. But this cozy relationship between state and religion had been allowed to bear upon the appointment of government cadres. Besides being from Central Vietnam, any aspirants to inner-circle trust and fast advancement believed it necessary to be Roman Catholic like the President. Position-seekers therefore began to read the Bible and convert to Catholicism in increasing numbers. Men of self-respect, however, refused to follow suit; despite this, many of them continued to hold key jobs. Naturally the regime could not force all civil servants and servicemen to adopt Catholicism. If such was its secret desire, this desire was never openly admitted.

The ascendency of military men to power after President Diem's death raised hopes of eradicating discriminatory practices deemed detrimental to national unity and the war effort. Since the RVNAF had always been regarded as a melting pot where regional and religious harmony prevailed, everyone expected the new leaders to set the example.

But the public soon found with disappointment that regionalist feelings were still strong and persistent. Once holding power, for example, General Duong Van Minh made no secret of his discrimination against non-southerners with whom he had no inclination to cooperate. So when General Nguyen Khanh, a native Southerner who was married to a Northern woman, deposed Minh on 30 January 1964, he enjoyed some popularity among the generals. Other civilian leaders who succeeded Khanh in power also seemed unable to avoid this common weakness. Mr. Tran Van Huong, for example, preferred to use only Southerners. His government, which was composed mostly of Southerners, did not last long because of this narrow-mindedness. The subsequent conflict between Chief of State Phan Khac Suu (a Southerner) and Prime Minister Phan Huy Quat (a Northerner) stemmed largely from regional rivalry. Prime Minister Quat had asked a number of cabinet ministers to resign in order for him to reshuffle his cabinet. Two Southern cabinet members, supported by Mr. Suu, refused to comply. Compounded by criticisms from religious groups the open rift finally forced Phan Huy Quat to resign and hand power over to the military in June 1966.

Regional discrimination did not just reign among government and military circles; it prevailed among religious and political groups as well. During the Buddhist struggle of 1966 the rift became evident among Buddhist ranks, which split into the militant An Quang faction led by Central-born monks and the Vien Hoa Dao (Institute for the Propagation of Buddhism) led by moderate Northern monks. On several occasions the schism between the two factions degenerated into bloody confrontation, and this weakened the ranks of military Buddhists. Things were no better for political parties whose ranks were also split along regional lines. There was no solidarity between the Central and Southern branches of the Dai Viet Party; likewise, there was no harmony among the Northern, Central, and Southern organizations of the VNQDD (Nationalist Party). Even party veterans such as Vu Hong Khanh and Nguyen Hoa Hiep were unable to patch up regional differences and unify the VNQDD.

From 1 November 1963 on, the problem of religious rivalry ceased to be a major concern but regional rivalry was still pervasive, though less visible. The stabilizing principle that seemed to guide every government after Mr. Diem was that the least trouble would arise if only native-born officials were appointed to local positions. This guideline also dictated that organizations at the central level (such as the Cabinet, the Council for the Preservation of the Constitution, or the Council of State Elders) should have equal representation from all three regions. Even in military organizations, commanding officers often tried to achieve geographical balance in personnel assignments to avoid being branded as discriminatory and curb the unsettling effects of regionalism.

However, there were notable and successful exceptions. The Northern General Nguyen Duc Thang, for example, had served as CG of IV Corps/MR-4. Generals Tran Van Don, Do Cao Tri, and Ngo Quang Truong, all Southerners, had successively held command of I Corps/MR-1. General Ngo Quang Truong in particular after leading the paratroopers to regain control of Da Nang and Hue during the Buddhist struggle of 1966 was appointed CG of the 1st Infantry Division in Hue. Another significant exception was that during General Truong's tour of duty as I Corps/MR-1 commander, from mid 1972 to 1975, two out of three infantry divisions and five out of six provinces and cities under his control were headed by Northerners; the remaining infantry division and province were at times commanded by Southerners. This was quite a success in a region where regional bigotry was reputedly strong.

While regional discrimination was a fact of South Vietnamese life, the game had its own rules. These were fairness and openness. Fairness required equal treatment and devotion to the common good and not the selfish interests of any individual or faction. Openness demanded that everything be above-board, unhidden. As long as these rules were respected, the problem of regionalism could be surmounted.

But if religious and regional discrimination could be gradually kept under control through conscious efforts, factionalism continued to reign unchecked in all areas. This acute sectarian attitude tended to consider one's own clique, group, party, family, or religion as the only one worthy of trust and preponderance. Such an attitude caused untold harm and was a tragedy for the Republic of Vietnam.

Under the rule of the Ngo, "our party" and "our family" stood above everything else. The party here was the *Can Lao Nhan Vi Cach Mang* (the evolutionary Personalist Labor Party), which Mr. Ngo Dinh Nhu founded and directed. The Can Lao Party recruited its members secretly and positioned them throughout the governmental and military establishment. Its strength derived from the fact that it took great pains to screen and select members who were loyal and frequently competent. But since the Can Lao was a government's party, it was not easy to prevent opportunists from joining for their own selfish aims. These black sheep caused so much damage to the Party that it eventually lost both prestige and attractiveness.

Family rule was a charge most widely leveled at President Diem's regime. But besides the President, only two of his brothers ever held public office: Mr. Ngo Dinh Nhu who served as Political Advisor to the President and Mr. Ngo Dinh Luyen, Ambassador-at-large to some European countries. Mr. Luyen spent most of his time in Europe and contributed little to state affairs. Mr. Nhu, however, was the eminence grise, the mastermind of the regime and the one truly indispensible to the President. It was he who charted the RVN course and devised major policies. In the eyes of the South Vietnamese people, Mr. Nhu and Mr. Diem accomplished exceptionally good things. Most criticisms or hatred, therefore, were mainly directed against the three other members of the Ngo family: Mme Ngo Dinh Nhu (maiden name Tran Thi Le Xuan), Archbishop Ngo Dinh Thuc, and Mr. Ngo Dinh Can, the youngest brother.

Mme Ngo Dinh Nhu was probably the most maligned of all. Since President Diem was a bachelor, Mme Nhu was elevated to the position of First Lady. Intelligent, quick-minded, and progressive, she meant to help the President and raise the status of Vietnamese women. Perhaps her excessive zeal was carrying her too far, especially in a society that by tradition conceived of the women's role as a rather inconspicuous one. Her imperiousness showed in the many ways she verbally dominated and even abused her colleagues in the National Assembly while trying to push through her pet legislations, the Family Code and the Morality Preservation Act. Mme Nhu was the first woman to launch the collar-less, open-necked *ao dai* (lady's traditional tunic), a fashion style that caught on sucessfully in Saigon. At the height of the Buddhist struggle in the summer of 1963, she was constantly lashing out at the monks with bitterness, cynically depicting their self-immolation as "a barbecue party." Her wry comments had on several occasions irritated even American officials in Saigon. Mme Nhu was thus the most controversial figure of the First Republic.

Contributing little to the affairs of state, Archbishop Ngo Dinh Thuc endeavored to enhance the posture of the Catholic Church. He built and developed numerous Catholic institutions. His faith and perhaps a little personal ambition were the motivating force behind his activism and efforts to expand Catholic power in a country composed largely of non-Catholics.[3]

The third controversial figure was Mr. Ngo Dinh Can. Being the youngest son, he stayed in Hue to care for their mother, Mme Ngo Dinh Kha. Simply on account of his brother's status, he became a leading personality in the northern part of South Vietnam. The Delegate of the Government in MR-1, major unit commanders, and province chiefs all came to report their official business to him and to seek his advice. A leading member of the Can Lao Party in MR-1, he ran business ventures there to finance party activities and also controlled a secret police network designed to eliminate the VCI. This police network was known for its effectiveness against the Communists, but it was also employed to suppress opposition. As his power grew apace, rumor had it that his personal prestige had put him at odds with his brother Nhu. In any event this power of his, which practically cowered everyone in MR-1, had been achieved only at the cost of widespread hatred against his person. No doubt his henchmen were indulging in abuse and excesses in a region where the people's hardship had become legendary.

With the fall of the First Republic the RVN witnessed a period of disruptive turmoil and factionalism such as had never occurred before. In the place of one ruling party there was now a proliferation of conflicting, quarrelling parties, factions, and cliques. South Vietnamese society, relieved of the constraints of the previous regime, seemed to explode in an uncontrollable paroxysm of activism.

---

[3] The Vatican was contemplating at the time the appointment of two cardinals for Vietnam, one for the North, one for the South. Msgr Thuc apparently aspired to become one. In the end only Msgr Trinh Nhu Khue of North Vietnam was elevated to cardinal.

In the wake of the 1 November 1963 coup, the following factions emerged: the ruling Duong Van Minh clique which was still dividing among its members the spoils of power, the Nguyen Khanh clique that staged the putsch soon afterwards, and the Buddhist clerics who had become arrogant power brokers. Different university student groups and Dai Viet activists also began to make their impact felt. Along with the Nguyen Khanh clique, the "young Turks" (Nguyen Chanh Thi, Nguyen Cao Ky, Nguyen Huu Co, et al.) made their spectacular debut on the political stage. The Catholics, still nurturing their battered image from their close association with the previous regime, became defensive and reacted only when absolutely necessary. The Cao Dai and Hoa Hao, watching from the sidelines, were content with their quiet little power niches. At the same time, civic groups such as the Caravelle Group, the Inter-School Group, old party leaders, and returned political exiles were emerging tumultuously onto the national scene, all vying for power. The South Vietnamese political arena soon turned into chaos. Individuals were pitted against individuals, students against students, parties against parties, religions against religions, and each against all others. Coups and counter-coups came in rapid succession. In the twenty months following 1 November 1963 South Vietnam had no less than nine governments, but none seemed to enjoy any popularity.

When the military government led by Nguyen Van Thieu and Nguyen Cao Ky came to power the situation began to stabilize, but not significantly. The victorious young Turks, barely in control, were already beginning to quarrel among themselves. Their elimination of General Nguyen Chanh Thi from I Corps command provided militant Buddhists with a pretext for the next round of disturbances that were to break out in Hue and Da Nang in 1966. General Nguyen Huu Co's dismissal, though failing to cause any major trouble, marked the beginning of strained relations between President Nguyen Van Thieu and Vice President Nguyen Cao Ky, whose alliance had been consummated in a marriage of convenience through the 1967 elections. This rift, when seen in the light of the subsequent opposition by General Duong Van Minh's faction, who enjoyed the support of the An Quang Buddhists, was truly the source of disturbing tragicomic events in the years ahead.

Civic and religious groups, who had been expecting a return to civilian rule, were clearly discontented. Political leaders, who regarded themselves as intellectuals, professed little respect for the individual worth and ability of the generals; they often had no inclination to collaborate with the military. For their part, military leaders prided themselves on their organizational skill and leadership role in the anti-Communist struggle and looked down on civilian leaders as "armchair politicians," or "tearoom-statesmen" who were both unrealistic and weak in leadership. Neither side seemed to understand the other nor was inclined to sit down with the other in a joint venture except when motivated by self-interest.

In general, the civilian Ngo Dinh Diem government, despite its ability to maintain a high degree of stability, had failed to produce a dynamic national unity. Subsequent military governments failed even more dismally to maintain the social order and achieve popular consent and unity. Apart from discrimination and factionalism, South Vietnam's social and political life was replete with contending pressure groups, among which the influence of major religions seemed to eclipse that of political parties. This was a phenomenon worth analyzing in depth.

The Struggle of Political and Religious Groups

To nationalist political groups operating in North Vietnam, the Geneva Agreements of 1954, which partitioned the country into two parts, came as an excruciating blow. Stunned by the event, the Dai Viet, the VNQDD, and other prominent Northern political figures banded together to found the "Committee for the Protection of North Vietnam" with the purpose of exhorting National Army units to resist the attempt to divide the country. They were rapidly overtaken by events when masses of refugees started to leave and military units boarded ships heading south. During their last days in North Vietnam, therefore, nationalists achieved nothing significant apart from dismantling the One-Pillar Pagoda in Hanoi, which was a revered cultural relic, and shipping out a number of anthropological artifacts from the Ecole Francaise d'Extreme Orient museum, also in Hanoi.

Once in Saigon, refugee political groups found their hands tied for lack of operating and popular bases; their southern chapters did not fare any better because of organizational weaknesses. At that juncture politicians from Southern religious sects were still wavering among several alternatives: support Bao Dai, collaborate with the French, support the new Prime Minister Ngo Dinh Diem, or just wait and see.

According to Mr. Nhi Lang, a key witness of sectarian politics during those days, while the Binh Xuyen affair was coming to a crisis and after Chief of State Bao Dai had just called Prime Minister Diem to France for consultations, representatives from eighteen political and civic groups met on 29 April 1955 to form the People's Revolutionary Council. Under the collective leadership of Nguyen Bao Toan, representative of the Social Democratic Party (Hoa Hao), Ho Han Son, representative of the Vietnam Restoration Association (Cao Dai), and Nhi Lang, representative of the National Resistance Front (anti-French Cao Dai), this Council decided to depose Bao Dai, dissolve the Ngo Dinh Diem cabinet, and entrust statesman Diem with the mission of forming a new government whose function was to hold elections for the Constitutional Assembly and to found a republic for South Vietnam. This resolution took Prime Minister Diem by surprise but gave him more leverage in solving subsequent crises, although those who had been instrumental in fomenting the bold move were eventually to find themselves as political exiles.[4]

After his victory over ex-Emperor Bao Dai, President Diem grew impatient with political opposition. From 1956 to 1958, remnants of the Dai Viet and VNQDD in Central Vietnam were quietly struggling against the Can Lao Party and its front, the National Revolutionary Movement. An army unit sympathetic to the Dai Viet seceded and set up a resistance

---

[4]"The Origin of the First Republic" from The Memoirs of Nhi Lang (now a refugee in the United States), Que Huong Tuyen Tap (Selections on the Fatherland), 1977, pp. 19-27.

base in the Ba Long area west of Quang Tri, but the dissidents disintegrated when President Diem sent loyal troops after them. Another attempt at agitation, undertaken by the VNQDD in Quang Nam Province, was also quickly squelched.

In April 1960 eighteen prominent figures met in the Caravelle Hotel in Saigon to set up a new political organization called the Bloc for Liberty and Progress and signed a manifesto demanding improvements in the government. The manifesto called for a more liberal regime, reelection of the National Assembly, and a government fully accountable to the National Assembly, implying of course the participation of the signatory parties. In November 1960 the aborted coup staged by military officers such as Colonels Nguyen Chanh Thi, Vuong Van Dong, Nguyen Trieu Hong, and Pham Van Lieu led to the arrest of one member of the Caravelle Group, Mr. Phan Khac Suu, on charges of colluding with the coup leaders. The remaining members of the Caravelle Group were also arrested; after this, opposition to Mr. Diem seemed to be completely paralyzed.

After the demise of the First Republic the political scene of South Vietnam came alive. Two and a half months after the November coup the Republic of Vietnam had no fewer than 62 political groups. Old parties had broken into splinter groups and new parties were quickly formed. Several political exiles returned from abroad and set about forming parties to contend for power. Inaugurating the Council of Notabilities, General Duong Van Minh expressed the junta's hope that the country would revert to true democratic practice and asked the Council to draft a new Constitution. The Council launched into endless debates and failed to accomplish anything. The Military Revolutionary Council, under General Minh's leadership, had been wanting to consolidate political groups into three or four major parties. Colonel Pham Ngoc Thao was entrusted with this mission, but his liaison with political groups towards this end failed to produce any result. The spate of activity by different groups on the political scene then bode well for the effort to build a democratic system. Ultimately, however, these political groups did little else than loudly criticize the government and denounce one another.

When General Nguyen Khanh acceded to power, he proclaimed himself free of political ties; yet the composition of his Cabinet clearly showed

Dai Viet colors. Dr. Nguyen Ton Hoan, a Dai Viet leader living in exile in France, had been invited home to set up a new government. Falling short of this goal, he finally served as Deputy Prime Minister for Rural Reconstruction. Two other Dai Viet leaders also joined Khanh's cabinet, Mr. Ha Thuc Ky as Minister of the Interior and Dr. Phan Huy Quat as Foreign Minister. Not long afterwards the Khanh-Dai Viet alliance began to show signs of strain. One by one, first Ha Thuc Ky then Nguyen Ton Hoan resigned their posts after accusing General Nguyen Khanh of holding all power in his hands. The truth was Dai Viet leaders had failed in their design to place their own cadres in the administrative structure. On at least two occasions the Dai Viet were involved in aborted coups during this period.

Skillful as he was as a tight rope walker in a hopelessly complicated political situation, General Nguyen Khanh could not fail to notice the profound division of the country. He summoned representatives of political groups and asked them to draft a statute for political parties designed to move towards the establishment of two or three strong blocs, which he believed was more conducive to the process of building democracy. His appeal fell on deaf ears because political groups in South Vietnam simply could not work together, much less arrive at any consensus.

By the time the Thieu-Ky government began its rule there was so much political proliferation that, according to a report by the Directorate of National Police, more than one hundred groups had been registered as parties or associations. The man in the street completely lost track of the names of political parties and their leaders. Many new parties had nothing more than just a name, a temporary office with a sign, and a few activists.

In this profusion of parties, only long-standing parties commanded some real strength. The Dai Viet (Greater Vietnam) had a following in the Hue-Quang Tri area and some other local chapters. The Viet Nam Quoc Dan Dang (Vietnamese Nationalist Party), or Viet Quoc for short, had a following in the Quang Nam, Quang Tin and Quang Ngai areas. The Cao Dai sect in the meantime was trying hard to rebuild the Vietnam Restoration Association, which had been formed in 1943. The Hoa Hao sect had by this time split into two rival groups, the Dan Xa Dang (Social Democratic Party) and the Vietnam Dan Chu Xa Hoi Dang (Vietnam Social Democratic Party). On their part, the Catholics had their militant force known as Luc Luong Dai Doan Ket (Greater Union Force), which was predominantly composed of refugee Catholics from the North. This was a homogeneous and strong organization designed to be the main force opposing the militant Buddhists.

Though operating under a single name, many parties were split into irreconcilable splinter groups. The Dai Viet had three main branches: the Northern branch under the leadership of Phan Huy Quat and Dang Van Sung, the Central branch under the leadership of Ha Thuc Ky and Hoang Xuan Tuu, and the Southern branch under the leadership of Nguyen Ngoc Huy, Nguyen Ton Hoan, and Tran Van Xuan. The Vietnam Quoc Dan Dang also had at least three main groups: the Southern group with Nguyen Hoa Hiep as leader, the Central group with Bui Hoanh and Nguyen Dinh Bach as leaders, and the Northern refugee group with Le Hung as leader. Religious (both Buddhist and Catholic) influence was significant among party followers in Central Vietnam and those Northern refugees affiliated with political parties.

At the province level, the split was also evident among local party bosses. In 1966 the Quang Nam provincial Nationalist Party apparatus had at least three main factions: the Bui Quang San faction (which controlled the provincial reconnaissance force, the PRU), the Nguyen Minh Huy faction (which controlled the Census Grievances Section), and the Ho Van Anh faction (which controlled part of the Rural Development cadres and PF). These three factions rivaled for power and often did not hesitate to use force to settle their disputes. Mr. Nguyen Minh Huy, for example, was said to have been crippled by a grenade, and Mr. Bui Quang San, who had taken part in local power struggles, was assassinated while serving as a representative to the National Assembly. All these faction leaders were seldom willing to discuss party matters together.

In mid-1969 with the prospects of U.S. force reduction in sight, President Thieu wanted to encourage more political activity. Taking the lead, he declared he would form a coalition of parties for the support of the government with him as the head. He entrusted Mr. Nguyen Van Huong, Secretary General at the President's Office, with carrying out the plan. Ten political groups and parties were finally coalesced into a league called Social Democratic Nationalist Front, which made its first public appearance on 25 May 1969.

At the beginning of 1970 Senator Tran Van Don, together with 14 other fellow senators, announced the birth of the People's Bloc, basically an opposition group. Yet the announcement remained just an opposition intent.

In late 1972 to set the political scene in order once again and consolidate his power at the same time, President Thieu took advantage of his emergency powers to promulgate the Political Parties Law which spelled out the requirements that every party had to meet to be recognized as such. Some provisions of this law, such as the one which required representation in at least one fourth of the total number of villages in at least one half of all provinces and large cities in the country, were designed to force small parties and splinter groups to join forces. Soon afterwards, the government-sponsored Democratic Party came into being. When the Political Parties Law finally became effective, only three parties met legal requirements: the Democratic Party of President Thieu, the Freedom Party, and the Socialist Democratic Party. All other parties had become illegal under the new law.

Over the years it seemed that nationalist parties were never able to regain their strength after the Yen Bay uprising. Generally speaking, these parties suffered from a basic weakness: they could not secure for themselves a strong popular base. The Vietnam Nationalist Party and the Dai Viet had some popular following after 1954 but were torn apart by fierce political infighting and self-interests. These parties' disputes over material benefits had somewhat discredited them in the eyes of the people. Most of the other parties, which had been issued from urban origins, seemed to have more leaders than active members. A few rare late-comers, such as the Progressive Nationalist Movement founded by Professors Nguyen Van Bong and Nguyen Ngoc Huy, were heading in the right direction but did not have enough time to develop further. In practice, political parties in South Vietnam were mostly eclipsed by the activities and struggles of major religious groups.

About 80% of the total South Vietnamese population (about 16 million in 1965 and 18 million in 1974) claimed to be Buddhists, but regular pagoda-goers were few and consisted mostly of women and old people. Before 1963 Buddhism in Vietnam seemed to be dormant and was clearly disadvantaged compared to Catholicism. After 1963 the Buddhist Church came to life with a manyfold expansion of activities through Buddhist students, young men's and young women's organizations which distinguished themselves for their allegiance and activism.

The Catholics, though made up of only 10% of the population, were well organized and highly disciplined. During the period of French domination Catholicism was favored by French authorities. Under Diem's rule Catholicism played such an influential role that Buddhist extremists became silently enraged.

Two other major religions related to Buddhism were the Cao Dai and the Hoa Hao. The Cao Dai had about two million adherents and the Hoa Hao one and a half million. After their unsuccessful challenge to the regime of the First Republic, the private armies of these religious sects ceased to exist, and both the Cao Dai and Hoa Hao lapsed into inaction. A small militant minority of these forces might have split from the rest to collaborate with the Communists.

There were other minor religions in South Vietnam such as Islam, Hinduism, and Protestant Christianism, but their impact on the national scene was negligible on account of their small numbers.

The immediate cause of the Buddhist struggle in 1963 probably went back to the twenty-fifth anniversary of Archbishop Ngo Dinh Thuc's tenure which was celebrated in Hue in late April 1963. For about a week, religious services were being held in Catholic churches, and schools were closed for the occasion. Catholic banners and flags were flying all over Hue and most conspicuously in the areas around major churches. Well-wishing delegations of the government, civic groups and organizations, and province and district chiefs converged on Hue by military airplanes to celebrate the occasion and present gifts. For days radio and newspaper covered these activities extensively.

Hardly had this jubilee come to an end when Buddha's birthday came along. As a reaction to the pomp and circumstance of the celebration in honor of Archbishop Ngo Dinh Thuc, the Buddhist flew the Wesak (Buddhist) flags in profusion. The majority of the local people, who passed as Buddhists though not particularly religious, wanted so badly to improve their religion's standing after having seen the fanfare of the Catholic celebration that they started to fly Buddhist flags en masse even before Buddha's birthday. Local authorities, citing an old law forbidding the flying of private flags in public places, ordered Buddhist flags taken down except in the immediate vicinity of pagodas. This order met with immediate angry protests but, owing to the wise intervention of the Interior Ministry, the affair was settled peaceably.

Though the flag-flying incident had been resolved, a group of bonzes led by the Reverend Thich Tri Quang of Tu Dam Pagoda refused to let the opportunity slip by without struggling at least for religious equality. On Buddha's birthday, Tri Quang gave an incendiary sermon at Tu Dam Pagoda on the government's policy of religious discrimination. Masses of Buddhists paraded through Hue streets until dark and converged on the radio station to hear Reverend Tri Quang's sermon which was to be broadcast shortly. At the radio station trouble erupted when the expected sermon could not be broadcast because it had been censored. The masses broke into vociferous protests, angrily bent on rioting and charging the radio station. Local authorities used military force to disperse the demonstrators, and in the ensuing melee a grenade explosion resulted in nine demonstrators dead and a number wounded.

At this point the incident threatened to become a major crisis. The militant Buddhists used every resource to arouse the populace, and Buddhists in other provinces and in Saigon also joined the protest. Reverend Thich Tam Chau, leader of the northern refugee Buddhists, and the Cao Dai and Hoa Hao forged an alliance called the Buddhist Inter-Denominational Committee to lead the fight for the protection of Buddhism. President Diem's dismissal of the Thua Thien province chief (also mayor of Hue) and his promise to punish responsible officials failed to alleviate the situation.

On 11 June 1963, just off the gate of the Cambodian Embassy building in Saigon, the 73-year-old Reverend Thich Quang Duc burned himself to death in front of the camera lenses of domestic and foreign newsmen.

This flame of sacrifice led to a trail of self-immolations by other Buddhist monks in protest against the Diem government.

While negotiations between the government and the Buddhist Inter-Denominational Committee were going inconclusively, the militant Buddhists continued their agitation. High-school and university students who demonstrated in Saigon and Hue to show their sympathy toward Buddhists were arrested. Disturbances broke out everywhere, especially in MR-1. In some cities there were indications that the Communists were taking advantage of the situation to create greater disturbance. As the Buddhist struggle continued unabated in late August 1963, the GVN took stern measures. The Special Forces and the Field Police raided and searched a number of pagodas which were being used as headquarters for militant Buddhists in Saigon and Hue. Many Buddhists monks and nuns were arrested and imprisoned. In Saigon, Reverend Tri Quang and a few others took refuge in the USOM office building and were accorded asylum by the U.S. Embassy.

Although the raids on pagodas and detention of the Buddhist clergy temporarily stalled the Buddhist struggle movement, they also alienated and exacerbated urban dwellers. The feeling of discontent against the regime, party control, and Diem's family rule was smoldering in the hearts of the military and opposition leaders. The self-immolations and world opinion also combined to sway U.S. attitude. These tidal waves of discontent swept the nation in the coup of 1 November 1963, which ended with the tragic deaths of President Diem and his brother Nhu. Archbishop Ngo Dinh Thuc and Mme Ngo Dinh Nhu, both on a foreign mission then, escaped a similar fate. Mr. Ngo Dinh Can was arrested, tried, sentenced to death, and executed.

The fall of the First Republic marked for the moment the rise of Buddhism and the concomitant guilt-ridden decline of Catholicism in South Vietnam. In early 1964 the Buddhists endeavored to strengthen and develop their organization. In a meeting in Saigon eleven Buddhist denominations agreed to coalesce into a single body called the United Buddhist Church. This church included the Theravada branch, the Cao Dai, and the Hoa Hao among others. Soon after his accession to power,

General Nguyen Khanh tried to endear himself to the Buddhists by creating a Buddhist Chaplain's organization in the RVNAF (similar to the Catholic Chaplain's already in existence) and granting Buddhist land to build pagodas and other favors. The headquarters of the Vien Hoa Dao (Institute for Propagation of Buddhism) and the Vietnam National Pagoda were built in this period. In Saigon and other cities, Buddhist organizations spread to city wards and blocks as well as throughout the armed forces with their Buddhist activities and Chaplain's services. Still, as if to wrest more concessions and favors, Buddhists were continually criticizing the GVN for discriminating against and repressing Buddhism as under the First Republic, although the Nguyen Khanh government sometimes went overboard to satisfy Buddhist demands (such as giving the death sentence to Ngo Dinh Can).

After the massive celebrations of Buddha's birthday in 1964 throughout South Vietnam, signs of strain were beginning to appear between the Buddhists and Catholics. In early June 1964, for the first time after the November 1963 coup, about 35,000 Catholics staged a demonstration in Saigon to protest against the government's favoritism for the Buddhists and repression of the Catholics. While the Buddhists incited university students and their followers everywhere to struggle against Khanh's dictatorship and the Vung Tau Charter, a serious clash occurred between demonstrating Catholics and Buddhists in Da Nang in late August 1964. An American hospital came under attack, part of the Catholic settlement of Thanh Bo in Da Nang was burned down, and a few churches were vandalized.

Religious conflicts spread to Saigon and soon demonstrations, counter-demonstrations, and fist fights occurred daily on city streets. While serious difficulties were confronting the Armed Forces Council after the abolition of the Vung Tau Charter, Saigon sank further into anarchy, and bloody confrontations broke out. At the front gate of the Joint General Staff the guards were compelled to fire upon fanatic Catholic demonstrators, killing several.

When Phan Khac Suu was co-opted as chief of staff with a consensus of major religions, the Tran Van Huong government ran into opposition. Prime Minister Huong had insisted on the separation of church and state and appointed a cabinet of technocrats. Both the Buddhists and Catholics opposed him, claiming they had not been consulted. Waves of hunger strikes and street demonstrations sent major cities reeling. In Saigon and Hue the struggle by university students and Buddhists took a slant towards anti-Americanism early in 1965; they heavily damaged the USIS libraries in Saigon and Hue. But Prime Minister Huong adamantly refused to yield to Buddhist demands. Finally, the Armed Forces Council had to intervene and dissolve the Tran Van Huong Cabinet. The Phan Huy Quat Cabinet came into being at a time when Buddhist power became overwhelming.

The Phan Huy Quat government included representatives from every segment of the South Vietnamese polity: the armed forces, the four major religions, and the three geographical regions. Now that the Buddhists were calling for support of the Quat government, the Catholics began to oppose it for the heavy Buddhist influence under which it was operating. They were particularly adverse to Quat's harsh punishment of Catholic military officers who had taken part in an abortive coup against General Khanh not long before, such as Colonel Thao and his collaborators, and for his dismissal of other Catholic officers involved, such as Rear Admiral Chung Tan Cang and Brigadier General Pham Van Dong. The Catholics claimed they saw the hands of the Buddhists in all this.

Dissatisfied, the Catholics launched a series of actions aimed at toppling the Quat government: petitions, street parades, church assemblies, and sit-in demonstrations in the office of the chief of state. Because of personal conflict with Chief of State Phan Khac Suu and Catholic pressure, early in June 1965 Dr. Quat resigned as Prime Minister and turned the reins of power over to the military. In mid-June 1965 a new government headed by VNAF Major General Nguyen Cao Ky took office under the national leadership of Lt. General Nguyen Van Thieu.

Both Buddhists and Catholics felt disappointed with the reemergence of a military government. However, they refrained from disruptive action because two civilian governments had collapsed as a result of their opposition, and towns and cities had gone through a period of anarchy. On the other hand the Communist threat had also become so serious as to require the direct involvement of U.S. forces. The new military government showed itself to be tough and capable of stabilizing the social and political situation. But the top An Quang bonzes kept attacking this government for its inept handling of the economy and excessive dependence on the United States. They demanded the establishment of a civilian government.

Early in March 1966 as a result of infighting and as an action against insubordination, the Armed Forces Council decided to remove Lt. General Nguyen Chanh Thi from his command of I Corps/MR-1. General Thi had been an ally of the An Quang faction, had a record as an anti-Diem opposition leader for his role in the coup of 11 November 1960, and was well liked by the people in MR-1. But he had shown disregard for, and contempt of, the central government.

The dismissal of General Thi aroused immediate opposition from militant MR-1 Buddhists. Demonstrations, strikes, and market shutdowns first occurred in Da Nang, then spread to Hue and Hoi An, Quang Nam Province. The An Quang bonzes denounced the government as being corrupt, demanded reinstatement of General Thi and a civilian government while the moderate Reverend Thich Tam Chau, head of the Institute for the Propagation of Buddhism, did not want the overthrow of the government. The militant Buddhist struggle eventually spread to Nha Trang and Saigon. In Hue and Da Nang, thousands of military personnel joined in the demonstrations staged by the Buddhist struggle movement, turning these cities into bulwarks of open rebellion. The I Corps headquarters, a number of military units stationed in Da Nang and Quang Nam, and the 1st Infantry Division in Hue took side with the struggle movement.

Early in April 1966 while the Buddhists were setting up a central committee to lead the anti-military government struggle, Father Hoang Quynh, the spiritual leader of the Catholic Greater Union forces, announced he would deploy half a million Catholics in Saigon to support the government if the Buddhists continued their opposition. For his part, to mollify the Buddhists, General Nguyen Cao Ky announced that he would hold a Constitutional Assembly election within six months.

By early May 1966, the Ky government had managed to meet part of the Buddhists' demands by issuing a decree establishing a committee to draft the election law. At the same time it also decided to take strong action to regain control of MR-1. In mid-May 1966, a Marine and Airborne contingent was suddenly airlifted into Da Nang; this swift operation succeeded in pushing the militant Buddhists back into two major pagodas, the Pho Da and the Tinh Hoi. As the Airborne siege continued, the Buddhist forces in Da Nang began to disintegrate.

The operation to regain control of the city of Hue was fraught with psychological and political difficulties because the militants were switching to an extreme anti-American stance. The U.S. information office and consulate suffered damage from mob attacks. On orders from Buddhist clerics, city people moved their altars out into the streets to block traffic while forces of the 1st Infantry Division deployed in defensive positions, but the shooting match never occurred. Governmental units including Field Police forces had to pay their respects to Buddha first before clearing the altars away. By mid-June law and order had been restored to Hue while Reverend Tri Quang went on a hunger strike and the Constitutional Assembly's election law was made public.

The government's regaining control of Hue marked the collpase of the Buddhist struggle movement. Key civilian and military personnel who had taken part in the struggle were gradually transferred out of MR-1, but the Ky government carefully refrained from imposing serious sentences on them to avoid arousing unnecessary anger. Extremist Buddhist chaplains were quietly replaced by more moderate ones from the Thich Tam Chau-Thich Tam Giac faction. Reverend Tri Quang, the controversial mastermind of the Buddhist struggle movement, had been on a hunger strike for 100 days to protest against the government and the United States. His ordeal was almost totally ignored by public opinion.

Why was it that the Buddhist struggle of 1963 contributed so much to the fall of the First Republic while the struggle of 1966, which started out like a wild fire, so quickly ended in failure? The answer is that in 1963 the Buddhist struggle had a popular cause and enjoyed popular support. In 1966 the situation was different; the Buddhists, no longer oppressed, struggled only to expand their power. Apart from a tiny body of fanatic, dedicated followers, Reverend Tri Quang's supporters consisted mostly of greedy opportunists who were trying to take advantage of the rising Buddhist influence of years past. Such a rallying for profiteering purposes quickly melted away when it was clear that there was no longer anything to be gained. Thinking segments of the population felt that the Buddhist movement had gone too far, especially insofar as it had drawn army units into a mutinous situation. They agreed that the government of South Vietnam had to take strong action to insure its survival.

Subsequently the An Quang Buddhists called for a boycott of the Constitutional Assembly elections of 11 September 1966, but 80% or the eligible voters turned up at the polls instead. Reverend Tri Quang and his entourage then shifted their opposition against foreign intervention and war and demanded peace. As the South Vietnamese people became more reflective, popular support increased significantly for the Vien Hoa Dao Buddhists led by Reverend Thich Tam Chau. When President Thieu signed a decree to promulgate a Buddhist Charter deemed favorable to the Vien Hoa Dao Buddhist faction, Reverend Tri Quang vowed he would go on a hunger strike till death.

The 1968 Tet General Offensive then came along during this Buddhist strife; it demonstrated to city dwellers the need to support the government in its fight against Communism. The Hue people, who had been through a most savage massacre at the hands of the Communists, saw this need more clearly than anyone else. From then on, except for some anti-war faculty members at the Hue University and a few religious people associated with the An Quang faction who were constantly clamoring for peace, the city's population no longer heeded Buddhist calls for struggle. Since Hue, the seedbed for the struggle movement had become unresponsive, the An Quang faction in Saigon simply could not go on with hunger strikes and self-immolations.

Because they had boycotted the 1967 elections, the An Quang Buddhists had very little influence in the first bicameral National Assembly of the Second Republic. So they changed their strategy by endorsing a ticket for the 1970 Senate election, and the An Quang ticket of Vu Van Mau won ten out of the thirty seats that had come up for election that year. In the House, the An Quang had nearly 30 out of more than 150 seats. The opposition by these representatives and senators combined with the gradual withdrawal of the United States created a great deal of difficulty for President Thieu.

On the other hand, during the time that the government was in firm control of the situation and proved tough in dealing with the An Quang Buddhists, the other religious groups, particularly the Catholics, were maintaining a friendly pro-government stance. However, if the religious conflicts and disturbances seemed to decline little by little, the ethnic problem continued to remain after June of 1966 a consuming concern for the GVN.

The Problem of Ethnic Minorities

The population of South Vietnam consisted roughly of 80 percent ethnic Vietnamese; the remaining was composed mainly of peoples known collectively as ethnic minorities. Excluding a tiny proportion of Indians, Pakistanis, Malays, and Arabs, who lived in the Saigon area and were engaged in commerce and money-lending, the ethnic minorities included the Chams, the Cambodians, the Chinese, and the Montagnards (mountain tribesmen).

Remnants of the Kingdom of Champa, the Chams now numbered about 30,000 and settled mostly in the Phan Rang area, with a smaller group residing near the Cambodian border in Chau Doc Province. Basically rice farmers, slash-and-burn gardeners, and forest product gatherers, the docile Chams eked out a meager living and never posed any ethnic problem.

The Cambodians, about 400,000 strong, settled in the Mekong Delta, mainly in Vinh Binh, Ba Xuyen, and Chau Doc Provinces. Most were peaceful rice farmers; a few served in the military or civil service. Having long lived mixed with the Vietnamese, these Cambodians were not far removed from the mainstream culture; they all seemed well on their way to being fully integrated into Vietnamese life.

The Chinese formed the largest minority group of all. Their population was estimated at around one million, concentrated mainly in Cho Lon (Saigon's Chinatown) and other sizable communities in the Mekong Delta provinces of Kien Giang (Rach Gia), Bac Lieu, and Ba Xuyen (Soc Trang). They were engaged in commerce, real estate, banking, rice trade, and rice milling. Because of their industriousness, patience, solidarity, and mutual assistance, they had achieved success in all branches of business, and held a vital role in the economy of South Vietnam (just as they are in the economy of other Southeast Asian countries). The naturalization law promulgated in 1956 by the First Republic, which made it mandatory for all Chinese residents to become Vietnamese citizens, first met with mild opposition but finally proved beneficial to the Chinese. With Vietnamese citizenship they were enjoying greater economic privileges as well as the right to run for office, thus gradually acquiring political representation both on the local and on the national levels.

Generally speaking, the Chams, Cambodians, and Chinese engaged in no dramatic struggles. The Chams did little else than quietly establishing relations with foreign Muslims. The Cambodians had demonstrated in Saigon a few times demanding rights as a minority group, but their grievances were all met without difficulty. The Chinese seemed seldom to have involved themselves directly in power politics. They were always paying off authorities and accommodating to every government in power to insure freedom for their private enterprise; they only mildly protested when confronted with harsh measures taken by the government. The greatest minority problem for the GVN was the Montagnards.

Well over 30 mountain tribes lived scattered over the Central Highlands, an area half the size of South Vietnam. Numbering about 700,000 people, they came from different ethnic origins, spoke different languages, and were far less advanced than the Vietnamese. The Montagnard main tribes included the Katu (near the Lao border in MR-1), Sedang (or Xo Dang, in northwestern Kontum), Hre (in the mountains of Quang Ngai), Bahnar (in the northern part of MR-2), Stieng (in the northern part of MR-3), Koho (in the Bao Loc-Dalat area), Mnong (southeast of Ban Me Thuot), Jarai (in the northern part of the Darlac Plateau), and Rhade (around Ban Me Thuot). Each of these major tribes sometimes was divided into smaller groups. In general, the Bahnar (70,000 to 200,000 men), Jarai (about 200,000 men), and Rhade (100,000 to 200,000 men) were the most notable tribes.

When the Vietnamese expanded southward, annihilated the Kingdom of Champa, and annexed the lowlands of what is now Central Vietnam, these Montagnards had been settled in the Annamitic Cordillera since time immemorial. Essentially rice farmers of the plains, the Vietnamese shunned the highlands and left the mountain tribes largely untouched. Vietnamese emperors were content with extracting from them token annual tributes. These were a form of tax in kind symbolic of the Montagnards' vassal condition vis-à-vis Vietnam. Along the lowland frontiers, Vietnamese governors erected a series of military forts, which insured security for the lowlands. In time these settlements had grown into trade centers between the Vietnamese and the Montagnards.

After their conquest of Vietnam, the French poured capital into development projects in the Highlands where tea, coffee, and rubber plantations were established. Perhaps to insure monopoly of exploitation of the rich highlands and to keep Vietnamese settlers away, French authorities organized a separate administration and defense for the highlands, which they named Pays Montangards du Sud (PMS, the Mountainous Areas of the South).

After World War II, when the Viet Minh Front had succeeded in seizing power, the Ho Chi Minh government proclaimed Vietnam as an independent and indivisible country. Soon afterwards the French returned and waged a war to regain mastery over Vietnam as well as over all of Indochina. High Commissioner d'Argenlieu once again made the Central Highlands an autonomous territory in late May of 1946. French policy had always been bent on severing Montagnard country from the rest of Vietnam and creating division between Montagnards and Vietnamese.

Thus, the ancient suspicion and distance that existed between lowlanders and highlanders were further magnified during French rule and continued until today. In 1950 Bao Dai granted a special status to the highlands, which he called "Royal Domans" and placed under his direct administration. This act perpetuated the separation of the Montagnard country from the Vietnamese state.

During the Resistance War against the French, the Viet Minh tried to win over ethnic groups of North Vietnam's Highlands and those of the Truong Son Cordillera in Central Vietnam. Many Montagnards had joined the Viet Minh ranks as resistance combatants. In 1954 when the country was separated in two parts, five to six thousand Jarai and Rhade cadres and soldiers regrouped to the North. Naturally, these people were to receive further training and eventually be returned to their native highlands in the South for subversive action.

President Ngo Dinh Diem soon perceived the importance of the Central Highlands and the role of the Montagnards in his nation-building effort. In contrast to the Communist inclination of granting token autonomy to the highlands minorities, his was a policy of acculturation. This was a euphemism for his effort to assimilate the Montagnards to Vietnamese life. The long-range need for South Vietnam, as he saw it, was total ethnic integration and assimilation into Vietnamese society. But the First Republic's assimilation policy seemed to have been executed precipitously. Vietnamese in droves were sent from the lowlands to settle in the highlands, and overzealous government cadres took a number of untactful measures. The Montagnards, still unfamiliar with the status given them by the Vietnamese government, felt disturbed and threatened by the influx of the aggressive Vietnamese settlers. To add oil to the fire Communist cadres came along with their propaganda and promises for ethnic autonomy.

In 1958 a Montagnard autonomy movement came into being. It was the Ba-Ja-Rha-Ko Movement, an acronym for the tribes that comprised it -- Bahnar, Jarai, Rhade and Koho. It was organized by a former French government functionary named Y'Bham Enuol. The movement was quickly quelled, and some of its leaders were arrested. Y'Bih Aleo, a Rhade leader, escaped and joined the Communists who later appointed him Vice President of the National Liberation Front and Chairman of the Ethnic Autonomy Movement. Another Rhade leader, Y' Bham, and Paul Nur, a Bahnar leader, were imprisoned and not released until after the coup of 1 November 1963.

After initial experience with the 1958 Montagnard struggle for autonomy, the Diem government became more tactful. Administrative cadres were instructed to study Montagnard languages and to be flexible in dealing with the natives. From 1961 on, U.S. Special Forces began to organize and train Montagnard civilian irregular defense groups (CIDG). Still, the animosity and suspicion that divided the Vietnamese and the Montagnards were hard to eliminate.

In mid 1964 another Montagnard autonomy movement emerged under the name of FULRO (Front Unifié pour la Libération des Races Opprimées or Unified Front for the Liberation of Oppressed Races). In a manifesto dated 1 August 1964, professing himself representative for the Chams, Rhade, Jarai, Bru, Raglai, Chauma, Bishrue, Bahnar, Sedang, Hre, Kebuan, Hadrung, Mnong, Siteng, and other tribes, the FULRO leader Y' Bham proclaimed the struggle to throw off the yoke of domination by the Vietnamese. The FULRO reasoned that since the Communists had waged war to destroy the Montagnards and the GVN was unable to insure their security and always victimized them, the Montangards had to fight for their own liberation.

Less than two months after this manifesto was proclaimed, a Montagnard revolt broke out in Ban Me Thuot which sent shock waves rippling through the highlands. During the night of 19 to 20 September 1964, about 500 Montagnard soldiers from five CIDG camps around Ban Me Thuot rose in mutiny, arrested and killed a number of Vietnamese officers and soldiers; they also kept a number of U.S. advisors as hostages and seized the Ban Me Thuot radio station. Here Y' Bham, the FULRO leader, denounced the Vietnamese for committing genocide and demanded autonomy for the Montagnards.

General Nguyen Khanh, the Prime Minister, went to Ban Me Thuot to solve the problem. After more than a week of negotiation through the mediation of U.S. advisors, the CIDG rebels surrendered, and the hostages were released. Prime Minister Nguyen Khanh had rejected the FULRO demand for autonomous government in seven highland provinces, but he did promise several concessions. Montagnard villages would receive farm land four times as large as the current area they were farming, Montagnard customs courts would be restored, Montagnard languages would be taught in elementary schools, the Vietnamese language would be gradually introduced only in upper grades, and Montagnard youth would be granted favored status in admissions to high schools, the Thu Duc Infantry School, and the Dalat Military Academy.

At the time when the situation in Ban Me Thuot was returning to normal, the FULRO leader Y' Bham, his staff, and a number of Rhade soldiers suddenly disappeared. They took refuge in Cambodia, perhaps still suspicious of GVN promises. In March 1965 Y' Bham was seen attending the Indochinese Peoples' Conference in Phnom Penh which was sponsored by Sihanouk (South Vietnam did not participate). Here he extolled Cambodian assistance and denounced the RVN.

The internal political situation in Saigon during the years 1964-65 was anything but bright. The quick succession of events and the rapid turnover of governments were upsetting every plan to accommodate Montagnard demands. In the meantime, the FULRO movement seeemed to be gaining ground in the highlands. Leaflets exhorting Montagnards to rise up were frequently seen in many places, but sporadic and scattered mini-revolts were dealt with uneventfully. In July of 1965 about 160 Rhade soldiers from the Nuon Brieng CIDG Camp northeast of Ban Me Thuot defected to the FULRO with their weapons.

When Generals Nguyen Van Thieu and Nguyen Cao Ky took the rein of the government the promises to the Montagnards began to materialize one after another. In July 1965 a decree was enacted that revived the Montagnard Customs Courts, and a Montagnard Military Training Center was established in Pleiku. But in September 1965 400 Montagnards in the Buon Ho CIDG Camp (north of Ban Me Thuot) were attempting another mutiny. Only a timely intervention by ARVN units managed to disarm the rebels and avert a bloodshed. After this incident Prime Minister Nguyen Cao Ky paid a visit to Ban Me Thuot with another package of promises: the administrative and military responsibilities for Montagnard areas would be turned over to native Montagnards and Montagnard candidates would be given preferential treatment for admission into the National Institute of Administration and military schools. A special office for Montagnard Affairs was promptly set up in Ban Me Thuot and placed under the General Directorate for Montagnard Affairs in Saigon, which was headed by the Montagnard leader Paul Nur.

Nevertheless, the Montagnard struggle movement was far from dying away. On 17 December 1965 FULRO groups revolted in the three provinces of Phu Bon, Ban Me Thuot (Darlac) and Quang Duc. They held the provincial capital of Quang Duc for a short time, occupied two CIDG camps in Darlac, and killed 30 Vietnamese including a district chief. These revolts were short-lived, however. After concessions, the government was now ready for firm action; the rebels were tried and sentenced to hard labor or death.

Soon the upgrading of the General Directorate for Montagnard Affairs into the Ministry of Ethnic Development, the presence of Montagnards in the National Assembly as well as in military and administrative positions, and the stabilized situation all contributed to making armed Montagnard rebellions a thing of the past. Furthermore, the GVN never ceased to extend a conciliatory hand to the FULRO movement.

In August 1968, contact with the FULRO was made. Granted immunity, the FULRO leader Y' Bham and his aides came in total secrecy to Ban Me Thuot for a meeting with government representatives. The talks continued in Saigon and resulted in further agreements. In February 1969 a FULRO group rallied to the GVN. An allegiance oath-taking ceremony was to be held in Ban Me Thuot under the chairmanship of President Nguyen Van Thieu, but at the last minute the FULRO group appeared without Y' Bham. Reportedly he had been detained in Cambodia by FULRO dissidents.

Since then Y' Bham was no longer heard of, and the FULRO dissidents at large collaborated with the Communists. In late 1974 a series of disturbances occurred in the Ban Me Thuot area. There were assassinations, kidnappings, robberies, and murders around the provincial capital and particularly along the highways, where the situation had become extremely insecure. Leaflets that had been gathered indicated that one Y Kpa Koi, a former Montagnard civil servant who had taken up the rebel cause, was the new FULRO leader. It was also reported that Montagnard groups were antagonistic with each other and they created disturbance to discredit the Montagnard Minister of Ethnic Development, who at that time was Mr. Nay Luet.

The GVN had always recognized the Central Highlands as a vital area lying across the Communist north-south infiltration route and inhabited by a people whose allegiance was still in doubt. President Diem's Montagnard policy would have succeeded if it had been carried out in a stable situation untroubled by Communists. With the advent of subversion and war the Montagnards had become more and more aware of the escalating promises by the competing Communist and Nationalist sides. The Nguyen Van Thieu government had much success in dealing with the Montagnards because it granted them maximum concessions. The new ethnic statute had given the Montagnards preferential treatment, so much so that the Cambodian residents, who had been virtually considered Vietnamese citizens, staged demonstrations to demand equal treatment under the same statute. The war had transformed the Montagnard country into a scene of hot contest. Most Montagnard refugees who fled the Communists had given their allegiance to the GVN, and many Montagnards served in regular as well as territorial forces in the highlands, but the dissidents chose to cooperate with the Communists. The Vietnam conflict had torn the Montagnard population asunder, just as it had the Vietnamese people.

The Impact of Communist Insurgency and Protracted War

The Communist threat to South Vietnam materialized under two forms. One was a war of subversion or insurgency which dragged out endlessly and eroded the fabric of society and the other an invasion from the outside which supported the enemy within and was designed to seize the first opportunity to deliver its decisive blow.

The enemy's subversion caused a great deal of difficulty. It was like an internal malady that worked its lethal way through the nation's body. Deep inside South Vietnam's society, Communist elements seemed to be gnawing at and demolishing its internal structure as a veritable fifth column. The menace was the more dangerous since the enemy had cunningly used the very RVN themes to achieve his goal. The National Liberation Front and the People's Revolutionary Party called themselves popular organizations speaking for the majority of the South Vietnamese and claimed to be fighting for national independence, for an end to "imperialism" and foreign intervention. Those catch phrases that they used such as "genuine independence," "fight America to save the country," "peace," and "neutrality" sounded big and attractive and seemed irrefutable to any concerned Vietnamese patriot. Moreover, the enemy's strategem was so insidious and wily that he succeeded in fooling the naive South Vietnamese public along with part of the outside world, including pacifists, leftists, and self-styled liberals who prided themselves for their objectivity and perceptiveness. It was this strategem which provided the material and cause for a protracted conflict between South Vietnam's militant and non-militant factions.

The enemy's invasion from the North seemed to be a study in perseverence. Though North Vietnam's strength was limited, it was enjoying a methodical, long term resolute assistance from the Communist world that firmly stood behind it. North Vietnam was a huge staging area poised to go all-out and seize the opportune moment. It was like a main character who acted as the impresario lending support in planning war strategy, delivering underhand blows, and emerging only when success was certain. As an official stand, the RVN's allies and other countries of the Free World which were staying clear of the conflict seemed to accept the enemy's rules of the game. From the very outset the contest had an air of unfairness about it all.

Inside South Vietnam the only people who knew the Communists best were perhaps Northern refugees who had personal experience dealing with them and nationalist combatants who were resolutely opposed to Communism. Democracy Communist-style was a kind of regime in which the Party was the leader who made decisions on everything and the people had only the right to consent (but not to dissent). By reforming social conditions through the leveling of property the Communists had in fact rendered the people equal in grinding poverty. When all were equally destitute there was naturally some kind of equality. In the new classless society the Party and its cadres were the new bosses, and the masses became the slaves. The Party systematically destroyed private property and concentrated all property under its control. There would be of course no longer any scene of men exploiting men since the Party had reserved for itself the right to exploit. But the Communist Party proved in fact far more capitalistic than had been thought. When Communist cadres put into effect their injunction of "three togethernesses," they were not trying to be friendly to the people but to establish greater control of the people. Their control was in fact so sophisticated that there was no room for loopholes.

Unfortunately, such perceptive views on the enemy were not readily received and understood by the majority of the South Vietnamese masses. Whoever presented Communism in such a light would be branded "propagandists." People usually turned a deaf ear to what the Ministry of Information said because they did not want to believe it. There probably lay the dangers of Communism. Outsiders, who could not imagine such enormities, simply refused to believe the GVN allegations. However, insiders who knew found it too late to do anything. In spite of testimonies given by people who had escaped from behind the Iron Curtain as well as from countries that had fallen captive to Communism since World War II, few had paid attention to them.

Under such circumstances it was not surprising that the myth of the Viet Minh being genuine resistance fighters as promoted by the Communists had a great deal of attraction. The feeling of sympathy which many people, particularly the rural people, had for the Viet Minh was still very much alive. Furthermore, our enemy had advanced new promises which suited the circumstances and were couched in most attractive terms. Mere promises for the future cost nothing; besides, it was often easier to criticize than to perform and more convenient to destroy than to construct. Communist regroupees in the North were later returned to their home villages to reestablish contact with and coax the local populace; and so their task of building underground structures was made easier. For those who were not ready to follow them, there was coercion or threat. By killing one person they had intimidated thousands. Those people who did not actively work for them had to support them with labor and private property or to maintain a passive, uncooperative attitude toward the government.

For the loyal cadres of the nationalist government, the Communists had a simple solution: assassination, or kidnapping and elimination. Each year the GVN lost thousands of village officials and rural cadres. The enemy terrorized even teachers and rural medics and naturally hated our information cadres the most.

To the GVN the key to popular allegiance was its ability to protect the people. Only in cities and important population centers, in areas where we had superior forces, and in well-organized villages such as those inhabited by the Catholics and the Hoa Hoa, did the people enjoy a true measure of security. The rest of the country rarely knew safety at all; it was often the case that our side had control during the day and our adversary during the night. Our outposts were numerous, but their effectiveness was limited. After late 1968 the Self-Defense militia increased its strength manyfold. Still, in a village the People's Self-Defense and Popular Forces were usually encamped in the village headquarters and extended their night control to only a tiny area. Our people were not well organized and not motivated enough to fight; our territorial intelligence network was virtually non-existent. The enemy's assassination squads and tax collectors seldom encountered opposition at night.

Over the years there were a number of areas which could be called pacified for a certain time: those that received priority of pacification by the RVNAF forces, those where Allied forces were active, or those where the enemy was weak. Such situations rarely existed for a long stretch of time because the armed forces could not remain forever in any one place. A major enemy offensive or the assassination of a village or hamlet chief in the area sufficed to make the results of months and years of pacification effort vanish into thin air; the achievements of the pacification effort were precarious indeed.

The rural populace, therefore, lived in a state of constant fear and uncertainty between the anvil and the hammer. Taxes had to be paid to both sides, but life had to go on, and the people continued going about their business or farming to make a living. From the outside the situation appeared to be normal. Regardless of whether a hamlet was rated as A or B, its inhabitants were usually subjected to two systems of control and continued to provide manpower and material resources for both sides. This was the reason why, during the RVN best years in terms of security and rice production, the cities were still experiencing a shortage of rice, and the government was forced into an import program.

Changes in the security situation had taught the people to be smart. The higher the intensity of the war, the more contribution the Communists seemed to exact from the people, who, though hating the Communists for it, had to maintain a fence-sitting stance in order to survive irrespective of which side should eventually prevail. The situation was such that over a period of time many village cadres, and according to intelligence reports, even some RF and PF outposts assumed a neutral position and merely gave a perfunctory performance. There were also double-agent village cadres who worked for the GVN during the day and reported to, and received instructions from, the Communist village commissar at night.

Nonetheless, the GVN still had plenty of dedicated hamlet and village chiefs worthy of being called anti-Communist heroes. But these people had to be on their guard at all times. At night they slept in the outposts to handle their defense; during the day every step of their activity was taken with precaution. Such a style of work became exhausting and arduous over the long run. How could a slip be prevented, especially when the enemy was constantly stalking those people as targets for elimination? During the war years, South Vietnam had lost untold numbers of good leaders at the rice-roots level. Those who had the means left their home villages to take refuge in provincial capitals; often this was a one-way trip. Soon the countryside was left with a nondescript, fence-sitting populace who watched the war from the sidelines and suffered from its destructiveness. And among them the young underground Communist cadres, who had been the plainest and most ordinary rural people, were now carrying weapons and waiting for the opportune moment to establish a new social order based on the precepts of Marxism-Leninism.

In the later stages of the war, especially from 1968 onwards, the rural masses seemed to realize which side had a worthy cause and was more constructive. From a psychological point of view, it was clear that they were favorable disposed towards the GVN. But the conduct of total war, the tactics, and the strategic posture of the RVN did not allow a reversal of the unfavorable combat situation. After the relatively good years of 1969-1972, the situation was back again to where it had been earlier, especially after the fictitious cease-fire of January 1973. The rural people once again saw that a noncommittal attitude was still perhaps the wisest.

As for the cities and towns, our rear base and bastion, how did the enemy approach them? Here he could not openly use coaxing or force as he did in the rural areas. But the very nature of the South Vietnamese urban society had provided the enemy with a number of weapons that he could use to his advantage.

The first weapon of significant effectiveness was playing the very democratic game of the wide-open urban society of the South. As a matter of fact, the enemy must have found that this game was not too difficult because there was no dearth of political or religious organizations opposed to the government. Therefore, through the long-range work of underground agents and their proselytizing and propaganda actions, over the years these organizations had supplied the Communists with a sizeable number of bona-fide activists. Under the Second Republic, opposition lawmakers were often the most vocal, and no doubt some of them were aiding the enemy whether they realized it or not. Among militant Buddhist bonzes and nuns, intractable politicians, impulsive university students, and cunning labor leaders, who could tell for certain which ones were true nationalist and which ones were not? When the government took preventive measures, it was accused of suppressing the opposition, an action disapproved by its allies and the Free World.[5]

The political and social life of South Vietnamese towns and cities was like a jumbled picture or a concert without a conductor and without symphony. For the enemy, it was not at all hard to infiltrate the intellectual groups, the literary and arts circles, and the press corps. South Vietnamese artists, journalists, and writers prided themselves for their "liberalness"; they opposed and found fault with everything. The regime was consequently besmeared, and every nationalist figure was handicapped by a tainted reputation. In time a true crisis of confidence set in because no one seemed to have the ability to lead. This led to the popular myth that only among the leading personalities of the other side were there any bright stars and heroic figures.

---

[5] During the First Republic a number of Communist suspects were detained only to be released under the pressure of public opinion. These persons, such as Nguyen Huu Tho, Trinh Dinh Thao, and Dr. Duong Quynh Hoa, later became key figures of the NLF. During the Second Republic, intelligence sources had evidence that agitators such as Nun Huynh Lien, Attorney Ngo Ba Thanh, Attorney Tran Ngoc Lieng, Student Huynh Tan Mam, and several others were associated with the Communists, but the GVN could not take action against them because of sensitive public opinion.

Even in the cities the enemy frequently resorted to the use of violence, albeit rather surreptitiously. Prominent and refractory nationalist leaders were usually targets for liquidation by the enemy. Sowing further uncertainty and suspicion in the already hopelessly chaotic political situation of South Vietnam had always been the enemy's strategem. But his inner-city terrorism was selective. Some South Vietnamese personalities such as Professor Nguyen Van Bong had become the targets of a calculated campaign of political terror because they were promising leaders whom the Communists considered truly dangerous opponents in the future.

Terrorism also helped the enemy's economic ventures in the cities. A grenade exploding in front of a restaurant or a small plastic bomb planted in the restrooms of a moviehouse became newsworthy incidents that appeared in daily newspapers as a reminder to the business concerned of their obligations to the Communist tax collectors.

Besides, the protracted war which the Communists waged in South Vietnam had enormous social consequences. Chief among them was the deep chasm that divided country and city. The countryside of South Vietnam was the major arena of contest and as such suffered unspeakable destruction. The rural areas were the warehouse of manpower and material resources, and the jungled mountains offered strategic avenues of approach for the invading NVA. Our opponents regarded the rural areas as a strategic objective to be captured, which was the reason why the RVN and its allies defended them at all costs. The participation of U.S. and FWMA forces with their tremendous firepower added to the destruction. Many villages were completely obliterated from the surface of the earth. Throughout the war, it could be said that no corner of the countryside had been spared the destructiveness of bombs and shells; many areas had in fact changed hands many times, and each time destruction was worse. The end result was that houses were reduced to rubble, innocent people were killed, untold numbers became displaced, riceland was abandoned, and as much as one half of the population of the countryside had fled to the security of cities, province capitals, and district towns at some time during the war. A small minority of rural people with resources adapted themselves quickly to city life, but most languished in abject poverty in refugee camps or as outcasts in city streets. When the situation seemed to have improved, the people returned to their home villages, only to flee again at the next battle. This process was repeated again and again over the war years.

The direct result of it all was that the rural people, destitute as they were, became even more miserable. Their way of life, which was considered as reflecting the traditional values of Vietnamese society, had been shaken to its roots. The ancient order seemed to have disintegrated. The villagers and the Montagnards alike seldom saw materialize the promises of our side and the hollow promises of the other side. Faith in the future dwindled, and the only remaining hope was to be left alone in peace.

On the other hand, the urban way of life was totally different. Before the war there was no great disparity between country and city life, but the war had changed all that. First of all, the cities were safe havens where people's lives were relatively secure. There had been a few enemy attacks against the cities but they all passed and were quickly forgotten. Then while the villages suffered destruction, the cities profited directly from the war. The cities grew many times richer because of foreign aid, allied soldiers' spending, and the consumer-oriented economy of the nation. Automobiles, refrigerators, air conditioners were hardly commodities for the average South Vietnamese, yet they abounded in the cities along with other luxury items. City dwellers made good money and seemed to live well in an aura of superficial affluence. The effect was that such a materialistic way of living always demanded fierce competition and sometimes devious means to stay ahead.

The urban petty bourgeoisie was so preoccupied with self-interest that it became too selfish. The urban way of life, which had previously been Europeanized, was now Americanized. Urban citizens from politicians and professionals to clergymen and artisans all eagerly clamored for democratic freedoms and freedom of enterprise. This egotistic tendency seemed to sit ill with the need for unity and sacrifice for the national cause. While the villages wanted security and were required to fight and make sacrifices to obtain it, the cities just wanted enjoyment and demanded more freedom. The leadership provided by the cities therefore hardly responded to the aspirations of the villages.

Another feature of the Vietnam conflict was that as the war escalated and protracted, the cities sank deeper into decadence. The urban society was gradually decomposing for its worship of money, its injustices, and its corruption.

The business community was the first segment of society to have profited from the war far beyond the dictates of ethics or social responsibility. Throughout the war the economy of South Vietnam depended on importation and consumption. In order to raise enough money for the war effort, all RVN governments had to allow a great deal of imports from which tax revenues could derive, which greatly benefited import and export profiteers. Inflation became uncontrollable; since prices kept rising, they encouraged an unparalleled spate of hoarding and speculation and even trade with the Communists. The period of direct U.S. involvement was truly a golden age for importers and middlemen while the poor became poorer.

Another group of profiteers consisted of the people who engaged in direct business with allied troops. Even the relatively high pay which U.S. agencies' employees made as compared with the much lower pay which South Vietnamese civil servants and private employees were making paled besides the huge profits which business people were able to get from dealing with allied troops. There were legitimate business such as operating shops, service contract bidding, and real estate rental just as there were questionable enterprises such as steam baths, brothels, drug pushing, and other illicit trades, which only aggravated South Vietnam's social ills. No practices were base enough or ignoble enough, so long as they produced the dollar.

The moeny fever did not only grip the businessmen; it also seized GVN officials as well. It cannot be far from the truth to say that the joust for power in the RVN political arena was primarily motivated by money. To many people becoming involved in politics did not mean serving an ideal or working for the good of the country; it was simply a means of seeking self-interest. Once power was obtained and with it the profits it generated, an uneven sharing of the spoils of office became a major cause of division among factions, parties, organizations, and the armed forces.

When a high-placed individual came to power, his underlings were immediately seen installed in soft positions, and a new business network was in place. The profits made went perhaps in small amounts to meet the needs of the faction but in far larger amounts into bottomless private pockets. The people of South Vietnam witnessed or heard about office-buying concerning profit-generating positions in the fields of economics, finance, taxation, and supply. High police officials and province and district chiefs, therefore, all had to pay a price which varied with the money-making potential of the office. Prices had been discussed of the offices of the chief of the Fifth and Sixth Districts of Saigon (in the Cho Lon section) and of the chiefs of prosperous Gia Dinh, Bien Hoa, Phan Thiet, Kien Giang and Khanh Hoa Provinces. There were enough grounds for believing that military positions, too, were up for sale, although not on a large scale. Positions that had to do with the issuance of exit visas, economic deals, supply business, and industrial, agricultural and commercial development loans commanded the envy of all office-seekers.

For some civilian and military leaders a notable money-making venture was exacting contribution from subordinates. Periodically subordinates had to deposit money in the hands of their superiors. To have money for that deposit the subordinates had to get it somewhere or somehow; and for every amount thus turned in they kept twice or three times as much just to compensate for their own efforts. The corrupt practices perpetrated by the commanders of the 5th and 25th Divisions in 1974 were only the tip of the iceberg. The non-existence of part of the RF-PF strength in MR-4 was another example. It was only a matter of course that when the upper levels were dishonest the lower ones became unruly. This was the reason for the venality of lower officials and such ills as phantom troops, decorative troops, and the misappropriation of government property.

South Vietnamese also witnessed spectacular smuggling cases such as the "Long An Convoy" case. This convoy of motor vehicles carrying illicit goods started from the Go Cong coast and wound its way through MR lines bound for Saigon with Military Police escort. Such an interregional smuggling venture, which required joint operations, had to have been masterminded by a very high-placed and powerful official. Yet the investigation just pointed to some lowly officials who acted on orders; the architect of it all remained immune.

Any discussion of the money-making fever that gripped GVN officials would fail dismally without mentioning the role played by their wives. It was common belief that the role of women in a Confucian society such as South Vietnam was humble and subordinate. In fact, in Vietnamese society women played an important role in the family, especially in matters of financial management. The first revolt against Chinese domination in Vietnamese history was led by two representatives of the "weaker sex." Since then many other heroines had appeared on the Vietnamese historical scene. In modern times, many women on the other side joined the fighting while on this side most women toiled hard, and in the center of GVN power the wives of high officials were engaged in making money for their husbands. Observing Vietnamese tradition, these high-placed ladies played the usual role of homemaker; now they assumed the additional role of business dealer in the name of their husbands. The high officials saw this arrangement with favor and conveniently pretended knowing nothing about their wives' wheeling and dealing since this, too, was their hidden desire. Naturally the wives' ability to make money depended on their husbands' clout. These ladies formed their own cliques, rivaled among themselves, and were a major cause of the rivalry among their husbands. Around each of them there formed a small court made up of influence-peddlers, common-fund subscribers, and money-seekers who more often than not were the wives of their husbands' subalterns. An indirect consequence of all this was that their opinions had an impact on national policy, military policy, promotion, and appointment. While the husbands pretended blissful ignorance of what was going on, their henchmen and outsiders in their chitchats seemed to be aware of a lot of things.

The financial success of government officials and business people during the war led to the concentration of wealth in the hands of a very

few who knew how to take advantage of a troubled situation.[6] In the
midst of general sufferings, they managed to lead a royal life with
their mansions or villas, night-long orgies, gambling sessions where
millions of piasters changed hands, and their enormous bank accounts,
of course, while their draft-evading sons were also enjoying themselves
and their studies abroad.

People who were able to survive economically included those who
worked for U.S. firms and agencies, the middlemen, private firm employees,
pimps and prostitutes. The people who hovered at the subsistence level
included low-ranked servicemen, civil servants, and policemen, veterans,
disabled veterans, and refugee peasants.

The South Vietnamese economy after ten years of implacable war was
in a desperate situation. Let the facts speak for themselves: the official exchange rate of the U.S. dollar was 35 piasters in 1965 and 725
piasters in early 1975, a twenty-one-fold increase; taking the 1963 consumer index in Saigon as base (100), in 1974 this index became 2330.9,
or twenty-three times higher.[7] In the meantime, during the ten-year
period between 1965 and 1975, military and civil servants' pay increased
by only 600%. In terms of equivalent dollars, an enlisted man made $10
a month, an NCO $20, a field grade officer $30 to $40, and a general
officer $70 to $80, including all allowances.

From 1968 onwards government and military pay was no longer sufficient to make ends meet. By 1970, that pay was barely enough for the
bare essentials for the first 20 days of the month; by 1972, it could
cover only 10 to 15 days depending on the size of the families. In
1973 in a survey of EM and NCO dependent households of the 3d Infantry

---

[6] When Tin Nghia Bank was closed down at the end of 1973 for violations of the banking law, a number of huge anonymous deposits were believed to belong to high government officials and their wives.

[7] National Bank of Vietnam, USAID.

Division near Da Nang, it was learned that 90% of the enlisted families had not eaten meat during the entire previous month and 50% had eaten fish or shrimp just a few times (in South Vietnam fish and shrimp cost far less than meat). Yet despite such misery, life had to go on, and the war kept pressing its demands for more sacrifice on the part of the underprivileged.

The effect of this hard economic life was that government and military personnel, cadres, and the police in the rear had to seek supplementary means of economic survival. Moonlighting such as offering taxi service on motorcycles, tutoring or peddling, wives turning into bar girls, and daughters into prostitutes were a few ways of beating the high cost of living. It was small wonder to see high school teachers and even university professors cramming several schools into their daily schedule in the same way dancing girls in night clubs hopped from table to table. They, too, had to try hard to beat inflation. It was therefore problematic whether to label as corrupt those lowly civil servants and policemen who asked small fees for their services in order to buy rice for their hungry families. They surely could not get rich with this small extra income. Meanwhile, combat troops were underfed. Plucking a fruit from its tree or catching a chicken in a remote village to supplement a meager diet was an irresistible temptation. The problem of petty pillaging among combat soldiers defied solution.

Even more miserable were other fixed-income people such as veterans, disabled veterans, and refugees. Pushed against the wall, they had to react. There were demonstrations by veterans in front of the Ministry of Veterans Affairs. In 1970-71, the disabled veterans started a squatting campaign. Empty lots and parks in Saigon and other cities were occupied by the squatters who set up their jerry-built shacks. The authorities had a difficult time trying to solve the problem. A number of those shanties were legalized, and province chiefs received orders to build housing for the disabled veterans. In the provinces, the disabled veterans organized themselves and appropriated for themselves other economic privileges. Refugees from the rural areas suffered more silently; they did the best they could to survive. While U.S. forces were still in the country, they were able to eke out a living; but when these forces had withdrawn and foreign aid had been cut back, the situation became intractable, and discontent rose.

Another serious consequence of the prolonged war was social decadence, a material decay accompanied by moral bankruptcy, which would have in time entailed profound social changes. The first problem was that of prostitution. With over half a million foreign troops removed from their homes and having money to spend and a sizable proportion of South Vietnamese soldiers from among one million men under arms who were either single or separated from their families, prostitution sprang up without prompting. Furthermore South Vietnamese towns and cities were teeming with the unemployed among whom were innumerable poor refugee women from the villages. Bars, tearooms, night clubs, steam bath houses mushroomed in the cities and spread out to keep up with the base construction program of allied forces. That was a thriving business which the Communists undoubtedly used for the purpose of getting both information and dollars.

Prostitution did not thrive only around allied bases but expanded almost everywhere. Soldiers on leave with money to spend never had to look hard to find carnal recreation. Along with the ladies of the night there were armies of pimps, gamblers, drug addicts, and thieves who set the worst examples for all impressionable youths to follow. Without realizing it, South Vietnamese society was sinking into debauchery.

Strutting in the footsteps of allied troops were two other modes of relaxation which proved detrimental to Vietnamese society: the drug problem and rock music. Before the war there were only a few opium smokers, a tiny few, who survived President Diem's campaign against the Four Social Evils. But when the war expanded and allied troops were directly involved, the drug problem started to spread; for the first time the names of marijuana and heroine were heard. The drug problem might have been part of a Communist conspiracy. Or it might have been the operational result of an international drug ring with a great deal of experience in finding new markets. In any event, drug pushers clung tightly to American troops; they were aided by an army of Vietnamese itinerant vendors anxious to make a quick profit.

The drug problem did not only plague American troops; it gradually spread to South Vietnamese towns and cities, especially after the drug market had shrunk with the withdrawal of allied forces. Some Vietnamese troops, performing artists, hooligans, and middle-class sons and daughters became drug addicts. In the high schools, talks about "pot," heroine, and LSD began to circulate. And youths secretly got together to get "high".

Rock was a kind of music that was not popular in South Vietnam before the war. But the allied troops had a need: that of relaxation. Therefore, Vietnamese rock bands quickly formed, started playing hot rock, later known as the "young sound," and multiplied fast along with strip-tease joints that catered to the allied clientele. As this music gained in popularity among our young people, Vietnamese songwriters began writing rock music, too. As a concomitant to the young sound, there came into being the hirsute hippy movement, the far-out fashion movement, and the dancing movement. All of this, which was totally alien to Oriental tradition, quickly became fashionable.

The urban society of South Vietnam was changing unconsciously. The war was dragging out inconclusively; death and destruction were visible everywhere. Military cemeteries with new graves added daily expanded without limit. There were war widows still in their teens who already wore funeral headdresses. The prospects of the military draft, war hazards, and a life of hardship were hovering close to every youth's consciousness. Bullets did not discriminate, and continued killing seemed to have no meaning. Deserters, draft evaders, and street hooligans were leading a fugitive and uncertain existence. The hopeless impasses to which drugs and rock music had led them turned some young men and women into a life of debauchery, of frenzied love, and of total abandonment. From the lower walks of life this weltanschauung spread like wild fire to the middle-class. In the face of this onslaught families still determined to cling to the good old morality were hard pressed to protect and educate their children.

In such a tunnel of endless darkness, everyone was frantically looking for an escape and seemed to find consensus in an "anti-war" stance. Each group according to its own view was clamoring for an end to hostilities. The motives for such a position were as varied as the groups that held it: to overthrow the government and seize powers, to change leadership, to vent frustration with a meaningless, protracted, and inconclusive conflict, to express revulsion at a fratricidal war, to express painful awareness of social decadence, and to express national pride by refuting the excessive interference of the United States in South Vietnamese affairs.

Leading the vanguard of the movement to oppose the war, reject the United States role, and establish neutrality was the An Quang Buddhist faction, which was represented by Reverend Thich Tri Quang and his colleagues, Ho Giac, Thien Minh, Thien Hoa, et al. This group had lay supporters such as Le Khac Quyen, Ngo Ba Thanh, Tran Quang Thuan, Duong Van Ba, and Phan Xuan Huy. Initially the An Quang seemed bent on gaining power for the Buddhists. But when that intention had failed, it turned its fury against the military solution and U.S. intervention. This group was perhaps confident it could negotiate a solution with the Communists by using the support of Buddhist masses.

Partially in agreement with the An Quang faction was a group of power-hungry, profit-seeking, politically vapid personalities such as Ton That Thien, Vu Van Mau, Tran Ngoc Lieng, Ly Qui Chung, and Ngo Cong Duc, who elevated General Duong Van Minh as their leader. This group wanted to reach an accommodation with the Communists and pushed coalition as the solution to the Nationalist-Communist conflict. In this coalition, they thought, only General Duong Van Minh had the prestige to lead the Nationalists; the group was therefore distinctly anti-war.

Another group, essentially amorphous but sharing the same conviction, included members of the intelligentsia, who, stirred by social conscience, and genuine concern, believed, however unrealistic and visionary they were, that an accommodation with the Communists was desirable. Among this group could be classed Professor Nguyen Van Trung and liberal Catholic priests such as Father Chan Tin and Father Phan Khac Tu.

These anti-war groups were sometimes articulate in their opposition, sometimes quiet in their maneuvers. Behind some of their activities, anti-Communist nationalists saw the hand of the Communist underground.[8] They made little impact, however, because most urban people had no inclination to accommodate the Communists.

Yet, in spite of their fear of Communism, South Vietnam's urban public hated the war because it demanded too many sacrifices. In line with such a psychology, South Vietnam's arts, which had been lyrical, romantic, maudlin, and escapist, took on the overtones of war hatred. Artists and writers were now inclined to depict the sufferings of war and social dislocations and formed a new anti-war sub-culture. South Vietnamese artists often styled themselves free, advocated art for art's sake, not for politics' sake. In their artful portrayal of society they injected the element of hatred for the war. Most influential of all were perhaps the anti-war songs of Trinh Cong Son, who was imitated by other songwriters. These songs did nothing good to the morale of the troops or to the maintenance of the fighting spirit among the masses. About 1969 the Ministry of Information banned anti-war songs, particularly those of Trinh Cong Son; a year later, however, the pressure of public opinion and the widespread popularity of the songs brought them back in circulation again. War songs, anti-Communist plays and literature which depicted the heroic fighting spirit seemed to be the exclusive fare of the Ministry of Information, the General Political Warfare Directorate, and a few newspapers supported by the government.

After the United States decided upon disengagement (i.e. Vietnamization) a series of important events occurred: the cease-fire in late January of 1973, the end to American military presence, the U.S. Congress's move to cut back aid although the Communists never ceased fire. These were developments which shook South Vietnamese society in its roots.

---

[8] The Nguyen Van Thieu government had repeatedly charged some lawmakers writers, newsmen, and labor union officials of having maintained relations with the Communists.

As a result of all this, when in 1974 the Communists resumed their general offensive campaign -- a multi-division exercise in mobile warfare to draw the remaining reserves of the RVN -- the country was virtually on the point of total exhaustion. The economic situation was crumbling irrevocably. Because of the insecurity in the countryside, agricultural production plummeted; imported goods dropped sharply for lack of foreign currency, and foreign aid dwindled. The skyrocketing cost of fuel brought motorcycles, cars, and tractors to a virtual standstill; and industries that operated with imported materials were on the verge of collapse. On top of the military aid cutback the shortage of manpower was crushing. As the level of violence rose so did the casualties and the need for replacement. Each year only 150,000 draft-age men were inducted while military and administrative losses (including the 100,000-men annual desertion rate) amounted to about 250,000. The ranks of combat units were thinning out. The material and manpower depletion occurred at an accelerated pace while the erosion of morale and the will to fight, which had been smoldering for years, was reaching its climax.

After President Nguyen Van Thieu pushed through, with pro-government majority support in the National Assembly, a bill amending the election law which would allow him to run for a third term and extended the presidential term from 4 to 5 years, the situation in South Vietnam became critical. In the summer of 1974, over 300 Catholic priests met in Saigon to submit a petition asking the government to improve leadership, reorganize the government, and eradicate corruption. In the face of government inertia, the Catholic "Anti-Corruption Movement" was determined to force a showdown.

While some opposition groups and particularly the press joined in the fight against corruption, the An Quang Buddhists remained on the sidelines. Suspicious of the political motives of the Catholics, the An Quang Buddhists chose non-involvement. The latent rivalry between the two major religions of South Vietnam, which were vying with each other for leadership position at a critical time in national history, could not be ended. The charges of corruption directed at the nation's chief executive dealt a fatal blow to the last sliver of trust which the armed forces and the people still had for the regime of South Vietnam; and the question arose as to what would become of this regime, this democracy, and this leadership.

CHAPTER V

The Regime and Leadership

South Vietnam and Democracy

Commenting on the Vietnamese character, many administrators during the French rule used variations of the theme "In every Vietnamese there is a mandarin." It seemed evident that monarchy and the mandarin mentality had a deep influence on Vietnamese society and on the life, psychology and aspirations of the Vietnamese people.

From the time the nation was formed until 1945, a period of almost twenty centuries, the Vietnamese had known nothing but monarchical rule and had come to regard it as inevitable. Dynasty after dynasty, the ruler remained invariably a king with a heavenly mandate (a mandate to rule in the name of Heaven). The mandarins who represented the king in every administrative domain were regarded as "the people's fathers and mothers." In the relationship between king and subjects there were no documents to stipulate the king's authority and duties, but the people's duties as well as the sanctions to be imposed in case of disobedience or negligence were clearly prescribed.

Not until the beginning of the twentieth century when contact with Western, namely French, civilization had been established, did a number of educated people begin to familiarize themselves with the democratic system of government through the ideas propounded by Jean Jacques Rousseau and Montesquieu. In point of fact, however, the relations between the people, the nation, and the ruler had already been conceived centuries earlier by Mencius who said, "The people are or prime importance, the nation secondary, and the king negligible." Even though traditional Vietnamese scholars learned about this precept, it was improbable during the periods of prevailing monarchy that anyone would have thought the people could rank higher than the king.

In spite of its predominant monarchical character, in the opinion of many, the regime exhibited certain traits not unlike those of a democratic system. For example, the mandarins who governed the people were all chosen from among the educated through fair and competitive examinations. With rare exceptions such as the case of Dao Duy Tu, famous for building defense fortifications for the Nguyen lords in their fight against the Trinh, who was prohibited from competing because his mother was an "ả đào" (a geisha-like songstress), every citizen, including the poorest and the lowliest, enjoyed the right to take part in the examinations. Extremely fair and strict, these examinations were practically free of fraud and government interference. The second democratic feature of the regime was that the people themselves elected the council of notables to handle local government at the village level. Village affairs were also regulated by a charter co-opted by all villagers. This traditional autonomy of grassroots government was summarized by the Vietnamese dictum, "The law of the king yields to the rules of the village."

The concept of democracy as conceived in the West first spread to Vietnam merely as a theory. Few Vietnamese at that time had a chance to go abroad to study and observe democracy at work. Therefore democratic institutions, the relations between government and the governed, the authority of the state versus the rights of the citizens, and other political practices remained just concepts.

Phan Boi Chau, the revolutionary who was in the vanguard of Vietnamese nationalism, typified the classical scholar reformed by an understanding of democracy. Initially he went to Japan to found an anti-French resistance movement and instated Prince Cuong De as the future king of Vietnam. There he witnessed the modernization process that propelled Japan to the status of a world power and saw that imperial rule under Meitzi was not necessarily an absolute monarchy. Then spurred on by the 1911 Chinese revolution, he changed his mind about monarchy as the future form of government for Vietnam and modified Cuong De's title to that of General Representative (President).

When Sun Yat-sen's doctrine of "the three principles of the people" was proclaimed and propagated in China, it had a profound impact on

Vietnamese nationalist revolutionaries living there as exiles. In time this democratic concept of the Kuomintang became an inspiring model in the minds of these revolutionaries. But in spite of similarities in condition between China and Vietnam, the Chinese revolutionary model hardly served the cause of Vietnamese nationalism. For one thing China was beset by her own weaknesses, especially her internal strife and the Sino-Japanese War.

In brief the majority of Vietnamese had only a nebulous idea of what a democratic system was like. Furthermore, books propounding revolutionary ideas from the West were all banned from import under French rule.

In the aftermath of World War II, taking advantage of the Japanese defeat, the Viet Minh rose to power in August 1945 and proclaimed independence, democracy, and freedom in a ploy to win the people's hearts and minds. The Viet Minh held elections to form a constitutional assembly, the first national assembly in Vietnamese history, in March 1946. In the elementary knowledge of most Vietnamese in those days, democracy was understood only in the most general terms, i.e., "all men are equal; they are masters of themselves and participate in the process of government by electing their own representatives."

In time the people began to realize that the concept of democracy advanced by the Viet Minh served only as a screen for their Communist doctrine which was yet to come to the fore. But those disillusioned Vietnamese that went to the nationalist side during the years 1949-54 found little that characterized freedom and democracy because the French, still greedy in their neo-colonialist pursuit, were retaining all powers, sharing some of them with a selected number of Vietnamese collaborators only when absolutely necessary. During this period, therefore, the term democracy was seldom used, and there was no popular demand for democracy on the part of Vietnamese nationalists living in French-held zones. Perhaps they were at this time more preoccupied with national independence than any form of government.

The birth of the First Republic and the ever-deepening involvement of the United States in South Vietnam eventually transformed democracy into a household word. In the process of building democracy, France and especially the United States served as models to Vietnamese politicians in their quest for a workable form of government. The ideals proclaimed by the U.S. Declaration of Independence in 1776 such as, "All men are created equal, they are endowed by their creator with certain inalienable rights, among these are life, liberty, and the pursuit of happiness," and those propounded by the Declaration of the French Revolution in 1871, "All men are born free and equal and should always be accorded freedom and equality," were the very thoughts the South Vietnamese wanted to be embodied in the supreme law of their land. In a message to the Constitutional Assembly of 1956 which was intended to convey certain ideas that could serve as a basis for a Vietnamese Constitution, President Ngo Dinh Diem wrote in fact, "All Vietnamese are born free and equal under the law; the state should provide equal opportunity for all to exercise their rights and to discharge their duties."

Vietnamese democratic thinking was thus patterned after the theory of democracy espoused by advanced Western societies where citizens had long been familiar with democratic institutions and life. But South Vietnam just emerged as a developing nation with little popular enlightenment, widespread illiteracy, and a burdensome traditional heritage. Hopefully, all of these constraints could be overcome with time, provided the country was left alone in peace. War, however, began to impinge on the life of South Vietnamese society with every passing day, and the crafty Communists knew how to exploit every weakness in our systems for subversive purposes. True to the spirit of the game, opposition political groups constantly clamored for civil rights and the rights to life and individual freedom while the Communists were ostensibly advocating the same goals. This apparent similarity of goals between the nationalist opposition and the Communists seemed to create in the minds of certain government officials the suspicion that those who struggled for these rights were either Communists or pro-Communists. The South Vietnamese government, whether under the First or the Second Republic, always tended to abridge civil rights, especially the freedoms of political activity, of expression, and of the press. Invariably, national security was invoked as an excuse to impose such restrictions. However, nationalist parties and leaders were unwilling to accept arbitrary and indiscriminate actions for fear these would lead to outright dictatorship which they abhorred. So they continued to insist on the implementation of civil rights that South Vietnam's Constitution had proclaimed. The daily *Tu Do* (Freedom) which was owned by North Vietnamese refugees of long standing anti-Communist stance, for example, remarked in its issue of 8 March 1958, "Citizens of a free and independent nation have the right to be protected under the spirit of the Constitution." During the same period a national movement for true democracy openly asked for the assistance of American and French public opinions because as it claimed, "We have never enjoyed justice and freedom; we have never had freedom of the press, freedom of thought, freedom of movement, and freedom of assembly."

Anti-government factions in South Vietnam were wont to compare the level of freedom in their country with that enjoyed by Western societies, but they seldom contrasted what our people enjoyed with the bondage in Communist North Vietnam. They appealed to Western opinion to exert pressure on the Vietnamese government for even greater freedom, oblivious of the fact than even in Western societies freedom had its own price and limitations.

Public opinion in Western nations, especially the United States, also seemed to have the tendency to judge democracy in South Vietnam from the familiar viewpoint of Western people who, with higher and more sophisticated intellectual standards, never failed to note shortcomings in our system. But then they also failed to notice the discrepancy between ours and the Communist system. The criticisms of foreign opinion, especially of the Western press, eventually reinforced the fallacious belief that South Vietnam really lacked freedom.

South Vietnamese society could be distinctly divided into two major segments: the city dwellers and the peasants. City dwellers had a much better material life and a higher level of education; they were therefore interested in the domestic and world political situation. As was true with almost all urban societies, they were frequently displeased with the government, especially the police or secret police whom they considered instruments of the government. Some readily supported or participated in demonstrations against the government each time an opportunity arose, but most just contented to remain vocal in their criticism. It was not surprising that anti-government newspapers or those frequently seized by government agents always seemed to enjoy a larger readership. Apparently opposition had become a fad of the times.

Peasants, on the other hand, were quiet, resigned as they had always been and took no part in the commotions or demands of urban dwellers. They were simply not interested in democracy, freedom, or civil rights, which they regarded as far-fetched ideas not directly relevant to their daily life. For them, who rarely read newspapers or listened to the radio except for folk songs and operas, these far-fetched ideas had never been an intellectual need, and political parties were all the same. Their concept of democracy was simple and down-to-earth: the government should provide security for the people, freedom from oppression by local bullies, a fair trial if accused, a minimum but decent standard of living, education for their children, and freedom from exploitation and heavy taxes. Under any government in South Vietnamese society the peasants were the ones who suffered the most injustice and enjoyed the least protection; democracy for them had lost much of its original meaning. Over the years democracy, advanced as a cause, had been the subject of so many unkept promises, so much manipulation, and so much disillusion that they came to fear rather than be excited by it.

In short the greatest weakness of democracy in South Vietnam was that it had not been conceived and accepted in the same way by people who did not share the same condition of life. War was also an impediment to the practice of democracy, and the need for survival often dictated the curtailment of certain rights and freedoms. The following fable gives an apt description of how South Vietnamese viewed democracy. Four blind fortune-tellers, who had never seen an elephant, were asked by the king to describe it. The one who touched the elephant's leg asserted that it was like a column; the one who held the trunk maintained that it was like a huge leech; the one that felt the ear contended it was like a large fan; and the one who touched the tail affirmed it was like a broom. There ensued a heated debate, but none of them conceded that the other descriptions were true. Such was the problem with democracy in South Vietnam; each faction had its own idea of how to exercise and implement freedom and democracy, and it was well nigh impossible to reconcile all these differing views.

Democracy and the Leadership of President Ngo Dinh Diem

When the Republic of Vietnam came into being in 1955, Mr. Ngo Dinh Diem strove hard to regain national independence and unity and build a free and democratic system of government. Eight years later he was overthrown by a RVNAF junta and killed along with his advisor-brother Ngo Dinh Nhu. The downfall of the Diem regime was regarded by coup leaders as a way to put an end to family rule and dictatorship.

No doubt, the Diem regime had been criticized for its police state methods, its mandarin character, its discrimination, and some corruption. These criticisms were based on hard evidence. Generally speaking, the Diem administration did not include any members of the prominent nationalist parties in South Vietnam. The first cabinet, which was founded on 7 July 1954, had nine ministries. Besides being Prime Minister, Mr. Diem also assumed the positions of Minister of Defense and of the Interior. Mr. Tran Van Chuong, the father-in-law of Mr. Nhu, led the Ministry of Economics and Finance. Chuong's brother, Mr. Tran Van Do, was the Foreign Minister. Another relative, Mr. Tran Van Bac, headed the Ministry of Education. Mr. Ngo Dinh Luyen, Diem's youngest sibling, was appointed ambassador-at-large.

This nepotism was even more pronounced when Mr. Ngo Dinh Can, another Ngo brother, was allowed to exercise real power in the northern provinces though he held no public office. Every important appointment in this area had to be approved by him, and he practically directed all governmental affairs from his residence in Hue City. Mr. Ngo Dinh Nhu, as advisor to President Diem, was the eminence grise of the regime; his wife headed the Vietnamese Women's Movement; and Bishop Ngo Dinh Thuc held sway over the Catholic hierarchy and laymen. For all intents and purposes the Ngo family was not unlike a super-government in the shadow.

In addition to the fact that most key government positions were held by members of the Ngo family, it was believed during the early period of Diem's reign that anyone who wanted to get ahead in the administration or the military had to meet at least one of the "three-D" qualifications: D for Diem but also for *Dao* (the Vietnamese word for religion), *Dang* (the word for party), and *Du,* a vernacular designation of a native of Central Vietnam from where Mr. Diem's family was issued.

Well-known for his devotion to Catholicism Mr. Diem had frequent contact with Catholic priests, and there was clearly mutual influence on both sides. Mr. Diem enjoyed the solid support of Roman Catholics, especially the North Vietnamese Catholic refugees who constituted perhaps his main power base. For that reason it was believed that Mr. Diem had expressly resettled these Northern Catholics in areas surrounding and along main routes of access into the capital to serve both as a political base and a security shield for the regime. Catholicism under Diem went through a period of great expansion and ascendency with new churches springing up almost everywhere. It was not surprising that many Buddhists with an eye on fast advancement had chosen to convert to Catholicism in those days.

Many believed therefore that Christianity had exercised too much influence during the Diem administration. Christian philosophy thoroughly permeated the personalist doctrine of Mr. Ngo Dinh Nhu which purported to be a political ideology capable of containing Communism. Although conceived as a synthesis of philosophic systems that had deep influence in Vietnam including Confucianism and some modicum of Marxism, Personalism derived mainly from the thoughts of the French Catholic philosopher, Emmanuel Mounier, who propounded it in 1930. Still it enjoyed little popularity because it was deemed too abstract, too recondite.

Though lacking popular appeal, the personalist doctrine did not meet with as much criticism and opposition as the Family Code. Advocated by Mme Nhu and signed into law in 1958, this controversial code prohibited divorce, which ran counter to existing civil law. Many believed that the ulterior motive behind this law was Mme Nhu's secret wish to prevent a divorce that Mr. Nguyen Huu Chau, then Minister in charge of the President's Office, was seeking against his wife who was Mme Nhu's own sister. Apparently, it was also her desire to impose a strict Catholic injunction on family life in South Vietnam. This code was followed in 1962 by the enactment of the Morality Law, also advocated by Mme Nhu, which was a copy of the Christian code of ethics. For this act Mme Nhu was criticized severely for her intent to enforce Christian morality in a predominantly Buddhist-oriented society.

The *Can Lao Nhan Vi* (Personalist Labor) Party was founded by Messrs. Diem and Nhu, who intended it to be an organization similar but antithetical to the North Vietnamese Communist Party. Most Can Lao members were recruited from among government officials and military personnel; they were often nominated to run for the National Assembly. Using Communist techniques, the Can Lao Party did not operate overtly but through a frontal organization, the National Revolutionary Movement. Can Lao members who ran for election, though designated and supported by their party, always posed as independent candidates to create the illusion of a broad spectrum of representation for the National Assembly.

The monolithic powers of the Can Lao Party inevitably gave rise to bitter opposition from other parties such as the Vietnamese Nationalist Party (VNQDD), the Dai Viet Party, the Socialist Party, the Phuc Quoc Hoi, and the Republican Party. Long victims of the Vietnamese Communist Party, the leaders of these parties were understandably worried about the prospects of suffering the same fate at the hands of Nhu's henchmen. To them the Can Lao was just a prelude to the single-party system of totalitarian or Communist countries. The ramifications of the Can Lao party apparatus in the armed forces and the predominant role politics played in matters of promotion and assignment also caused a great deal of discontent among military leaders because the normal channels of command and military hierarchy were upset, especially in units with a large Can Lao membership. Servicemen affiliated with the Can Lao also were promoted ahead of others. In many units stationed in MR-1 there was the situation where an NCO, who was a Can Lao member, actually controlled the unit from behind the scenes; it was he who gave instructions to the unit commander in the name of the party.

Under President Diem's leadership, regionalism came to a head. The public usually scrutinized his successive cabinets for the geographic distribution of positions held. Native Southerners felt that their representation in the government was not always proportionate to their numbers. For example, many province chiefs in the Mekong Delta, whose population was overwhelmingly Southern-born, were either natives of North or Central Vietnam. Discrimination on the basis of region eventually flourished as a result of Mr. Diem's policy and remained embedded in South Vietnam's social and political life. Subsequent regimes after him found with dismay the same situation intact and even more serious than before.

The Diem regime was criticized as a police state because of the profusion of arrests that occurred during that time. The Presidential Political Studies Service headed by Dr. Tran Kim Tuyen and the Special Action group of Central Vietnam under Mr. Ngo Dinh Can were two secret police organizations which operated actively not just against the Viet Cong Infrastructure (VCI) but also against nationalist members of the opposition. The unfettered operations and high-handed methods of these organizations prompted warnings from many circles. In the 15 March 1958 issue of the daily *Thoi Luan*, its publisher, Mr. Nghiem Xuan Thien, alerted the public to "the threat posed by Diem's policies that alienated the people." Mr. Diem, irate, ordered him sentenced to ten months in prison, seized the offending newspaper issue, and suspended its publication. On 26 April 1960 a group of eighteen prominent political figures, known as the Caravelle Group addressed an open letter to Diem, warning him of the dangers of continuing with his current policies. Instead of heeding their constructive advice, Mr. Diem ordered all of them prosecuted.[1] The unsuccessful coup staged by Colonel Nguyen Chanh Thi several months later was perhaps the most serious warning to Diem to institute broad reforms. But the only thing that ensued was a fearful purge that rocked the ranks of the RVNAF.

---

[1] Mr. Nguyen Tuong Tam, a prominent nationalist leader and famous writer, refused to submit to Diem's justice. On the eve of his trial, 7 July 1960, he committed suicide, leaving a note in which he said, "My life can only be judged by History."

There were also criticisms that Diem's policies had turned administrative cadres into yes-men who were short on competence but long on glowing reports. A case in point was the Vi Thanh-Hoa Luu Agroville in Chuong Thien Province. Formerly under Communist control, the area had been rebuilt with government support and now boasted of numerous new homes, markets full of goods, luxuriant vegetation, schools, and a bus and boat system to provide convenient links with other communities. On the opening day guests and dignitaries were all amazed by the unprecedented success of this program. However, this outlook of prosperity did not survive long after the opening day because the people and goods that the local government had trucked in from neighboring communities had to be returned, and lush fruit trees, such as banana and mango trees that had been hastily transplanted from elsewhere for the day, soon perished for lack of care.

For all the shortcomings of the regime, it was a real tragedy for South Vietnam that this regime had been brought down by religious grievances, whether justified or unjustified. To combat Communism, religion had intentionally been made a dominating force on the South's political scene. But instead of reinforcing the regime, it had inadvertently unleashed the forces that doomed its very existence. It was the rivalry between the two major religions, Buddhism and Roman Catholicism, that had been so decisively instrumental in bringing about the downfall of Diem's regime. Both should be held accountable for it. The Roman Catholic Church, because of its excessive support of Mr. Diem, had unwittingly ruined him while the Buddhist Church, for its adamant opposition to him, had encouraged and contributed to his destruction.

The 8th day of May 1963 was the fateful day the Buddhists initiated their opposition campaign under the pretext of governmental repression against Buddhism. As mentioned in the preceding chapter, it started as a simple protest against a government order banning the flying of Buddhist flags on Buddha's birthday. However, when a grenade accidentally exploded during a Buddhist staged demonstration in Hue, killing eight people, events quickly unfolded and crystallized into a crisis of international proportions. The rumor persisted that local authorities had perpetrated the action.

Despite its tragic impact, the Buddhists' opposition to Mr. Diem in 1963 was much less intense than their struggle against the Thieu-Ky regime in 1966. In both instances the movement was led by a small number of extremists, Central-born Buddhist monks whose leader was the Reverend (Thich) Tri Quang. What kind of person Tri Quang was would be left for history to elucidate on the basis of his actions. Most South Vietnamese only knew that Tri Quang was a highly ambitious priest, which was very un-Buddhistlike. Before the Buddhist outbreak of 1963 few Buddhists knew who Tri Quang was or whether he had any connection with the Communists as suspected. Although there was no evidence to confirm this suspicion, hardly anyone in the South could deny that his political actions had been beneficial to the subversive designs of Hanoi. It was only known that under French rule Tri Quang had been arrested twice for being a Communist suspect. Later he joined his teacher, the Reverend Thich Tri Do, whom Ho Chi Minh had made a member of the Viet Minh National Assembly apparently to assume control over Northern Buddhists. After 1945 Tri Quang went to Hanoi where two of his brothers worked for the Viet Minh government. Upon his return he told some people he had "learned Marxism." Though residing in Hue, Tri Quang had at times mysteriously disappeared from the city, the last time in 1959 coinciding with Hanoi's stepped up subversive actions in the South.

Who had drawn up agitation plans for Tri Quang? It was known only that these plans were extremely sophisticated and pernicious. At the height of the 1963 crisis many suspected that Tri Quang's agitation could be fatal to the country. Buddhists from Thailand, Ceylon, and Burma cabled their protests against Tri Quang's actions which they believed discredited International Buddhism. They advised Vietnamese to eliminate Tri Quang from the Buddhist church and Vietnamese Buddhists to stay away from politics. Among foreign correspondents present in South Vietnam at that time who had witnessed Tri Quang's dangerous game, the most perceptive was perhaps Marguerite Higgins, who exposed the sinister and subversive character of Tri Quang in her book *Our Vietnam Nightmare*, published by Harper and Row in 1965.

Then the most serious disturbances came between 25 August 1964 and 1 November 1964, during which time Tri Quang hurled fanatic university students into waves of demonstrations against Nguyen Khanh, forcing him to seek refuge in Dalat. By his manipulations also Tri Quang had managed to create some bloody confrontations between Buddhists and Catholics during that time.

During the 1966 Buddhist struggle movement, Tri Quang's plans for the most part just called for a return to civilian rule. This seemed to be a reasonable demand, but the actions spoke differently. For example, Buddhist demonstrations of a distinctly anti-American character had been staged in conjunction with those calling for peace. Thich Thien Minh, a capable henchman of Tri Quang's, once declared in his sermons at An Quang Pagoda that the An Quang faction was willing to open talks with the NLF to establish a coalition government. Then, for the first time in the history of Buddhism, Tri Quang incited the Buddhist population in Da Nang to display their altars in the streets to obstruct military vehicles moving to quell rebellious units; it was also Tri Quang who ordered the burning of the American consulate in Hue. Through these and other actions, Tri Quang had effectively fashioned for himself a leading role among extremist Buddhists. Eventually a number of power-hungry intellectuals came to join him, thinking that perhaps someday he would write the history of South Vietnam. A striking example was lawyer Vu Van Mau who, along with nine other opportunists, was elected to the Upper House of South Vietnam's legislature on a slate representing the An Quang Buddhist faction.

No one could say for sure what South Vietnam's situation would have been like if Mr. Diem had not been overthrown. But an objective assessment of various leaders who succeeded him to power after 1963 indicated that Mr. Diem at least possessed certain invaluable leadership qualities that no one else had. The people's respect for his person was evident in the fact that he was addressed and referred to as Cu (Venerable) Diem or Tong Thong (President) Diem but not the belittling Ong (Mr.) Diem as some leaders had come to be called later. President Johnson, when still a senator, praised him as "the Winston Churchill of Asia." He had earned this respect or eminence, whether or not one criticized him for his errors or disapproved of his policies. No one, however, dared accuse him of corruption because he was a man of moral excellence totally impervious to worldly pleasures, and his religiously ascetic life was too well known. Mr. Diem also had certain traits of character which some elderly persons enjoyed comparing with those of Ho Chi Minh. Like Ho, for example, he was imbued with revolutionary ideals, gave up position and wealth, and led a life of celibacy. The personal prestige of a leader was paramount in Vietnamese society whether North or South. For this reason, Ho Chi Minh had created a number of myths about his person to win the respect and trust of the Northern population. But Mr. Diem hardly needed any myths to win his.

If some artifices had been initially used to elevate his person, it was because Mr. Diem was faced with a difficult situation when he returned to the country in 1954. Few Southerners knew about him. The South, with its feudal rivalries, paid more attention to local powers such as those enjoyed by the Cao Dai, Hoa Hao, or Binh Xuyen groups than to the central government; at best people only had vague ideas about the nation's new leader. For this reason provincial and district cadres who called on villages usually carried Mr. Diem's picture along to allow the people to see his face and identify it with his name. In order to further enhance the prestige of the nation's leader, the government required audiences at movie houses, theaters, or offical ceremonies to stand at attention and listen to the national anthem along with the "Hail-to-President-Ngo" song. The President enjoyed the awe of at least his collaborators. According to one witness, an academician had, after an interview with him, stumbled upon an antique vase in the palace because he was walking backward, not daring to turn his back on Mr. Diem on the way out. General Le Van Ty, Chief of the Joint General Staff, had to dry his face constantly with a handkerchief while talking with the President on the phone, so intense were his feelings.

Though his regime had been condemned for its regional character, the truth was probably that on his return in 1954 after many years of self-exile he knew only a restricted circle of old acquaintances from Central Vietnam and admirers from the North. However, he cherished talents and looked for them. When he heard about a capable person he would ask him to call at the palace so that he could evaluate his capabilities and personality before entrusting him with a responsible

position. These people were sometimes as lowly as district chiefs, for
instance. But this presidential attention to lower-level personnel made
them proud and spurred them to work harder at the job being assigned.
Province and district chiefs were known to worry when setting out on a
field operation because the unfortunate loss of a simple automatic rifle
or M-60 mortar would be cause enough for a reprimand coming a few days
later from the Presidential Special Staff, saying "the President is not
pleased because ...". Some critics held that such attention to small
matters kept him away from more important ones. But it seemed that Diem
had deliberately attempted in this way to teach all echelons, high or
low, a method of operation, a measure of discipline, or a sense of
responsibility and at the same time to create the psychological impact
of an omniscient leadership.

National authority was one of the three key areas of concern for
Mr. Diem during his tenure of office. National authority had to manifest
itself through national laws, a strong national government, and a unified
military establishment. For this reason Mr. Diem was determined to
dismantle all dissident religious sects and their forces as well as the
Binh Xuyen organization. At first U.S. pressure forced him to welcome
eight representatives from the Cao Dai and Hoa Hao, four from each sect,
into his government, including General Tran Van Soai of the Hoa Hao who
was appointed minister without portfolio. But these forces continued to
challenge his authority, and in March 1955 banded together in a Unified
Front of Nationalist Forces. The Front advanced a demand to reorganize
the government and entrust national leadership to a five-man committee
which was to include Mr. Diem. Taking this as a lesson from his accommodation with pressure groups, he was later adamant about appointing only
technocrats to serve in his future cabinets.

Though condemned as dictatorial, Mr. Diem started out solving
problems in a democratic manner. Press censorship was imposed only on
foreign-owned newspapers in the country or imported foreign papers. He
had probably seen the dangers of a controlled press, and found a rather
sophisticated way to exercise control. His technique was to remove
publishing licenses from private individuals and give them to the
Veterans' Association under the pretext of helping out veterans. In

return, the association helped him control the press by delaying the publication of any issue the government did not want to circulate. This showed that Mr. Diem, who was sensitive about criticism against his regime, had skilfully handled the press by shunning the harsher methods of seizing and fining.

The National Assembly elections of 1955 in the South were held with the fairness of democratic electoral procedures. Candidates of the opposition or independent parties had the right to nominate their representatives to the electoral campaign committee. They enjoyed the freedom to speak to the people in public places, the privilege to use the government radio and mobile PA trucks, and the right to publicize their platforms in any newspaper of their choice. However, there was a rule requiring that any candidate who received less than five percent of the votes had to reimburse all campaign costs to the national election fund. This rule was subsequently abolished when it was criticized as a ploy to eliminate less wealthy or opposition candidates.

Despite this the National Assembly under Mr. Diem came under attack as being a rubber-stamp organization dominated by the executive branch. This was a rather severe judgment because not only Mr. Diem but any chief executive of any nation would find it desirable to control the legislature and win its support for his own policies. The truth was that subsequent national assemblies in South Vietnam, though including more opposition leaders, had not helped improve national leadership or democracy; instead; internal division and antagonism between the executive and legislative only worsened the democratic process and diminished the people's confidence.

Mr. Diem's abolition of the village's council of notables and his granting of appointment powers to district chiefs in 1956 were attacked as a retreat from democracy. Yet the instability of the rural situation and threats of Communist resurgence had made this measure a necessity to guard against Communist infiltration into, and control of, the RVN's infrastructure. To Mr. Diem, rural areas were all-important. His concern about the peasantry was highlighted by a land reform program which sought to confer land ownership to destitute peasants and bring about more justice in land rents. Decree No. 2 of 8 January 1955 and Decree

No. 7 of 5 February 1955 laid a foundation for the new agrarian law, according to which land ownership was limited to 100 hectares. All surplus land was bought by the government for resale to farmers who had tilled the land for two years, veterans, refugees, and the unemployed. Before this reform, 2.5 percent of landowners owned in excess of 50 hectares, and less than half of the farmland in the South was actually cultivated. Farmland owned by French individuals and companies was extensive; for example the Domaine Agricole de l'Ouest alone owned 20,000 hectares. Mr. Diem regarded land reform as a democratic revolution much needed for rural South Vietnam.

Rural security requirements led to the establishment of agrovilles, pioneer settlement areas, and strategic hamlets. These programs ran into opposition and criticism from many quarters, ranging from politicians through popular reaction to Communist activists. But leaving aside errors such as forced displacements and the selection of resettlement locations unsuitable for a living, at least the strategic hamlet program had served as a basis for the pacification and rural development program of later years.

Land reform and putting fallow land to work (approximately 1.3 million hectares of farmland had been left uncultivated during the 1946-54 war) were Mr. Diem's means to achieve the economic goal of resuming exportation of rice. As a result of his efforts, in 1956 about 200,000 tons of rice were exported. Economic self-sufficiency was another objective sought by Mr. Diem. Consequently, despite U.S. disapproval in view of the security situation, Mr. Diem reactivated the Nong Son coal mine in the hope of producing about 15,000 metric tons a year. Then he successively built the Ha Tien cement plant with a capacity of 250,000 metric tons, a paper mill with an 18,000-ton capacity, a sugar factory, a watch-assembly plant, a motorcycle-assembly plant, a fertilizer plant, and a plastic factory. A self-reliant man, Mr. Diem much preferred economic self-sufficiency over dependence on American aid.

Though admitting the necessity of American aid and its role in preventing South Vietnam's collapse after the conclusion of the Geneva Agreements in 1954, Mr. Diem considered the preservation of national sovereignty as absolutely essential since this symbolized the South's independence, which was not only a just cause but also a burning issue for the South Vietnamese people. Therefore, although the presence of 270,000 French troops was contributing to the local economy, Mr. Diem insisted that they should be withdrawn from the South within two years as stipulated by the Geneva Agreements. In a further move to assert national independence and sovereign power, Mr. Diem enacted the Nationality Act and legislation forbidding the exercise of 11 vital occupations, both of which were directed against the Chinese who had been living in Vietnam for generations and who were dominating South Vietnam's economy. Many were of the opinion that Mr. Diem's insistence on replacing Chinese or French store signs by Vietnamese ones, the forced naturalization of the Chinese, and the introduction of the Vietnamese language as a mandatory subject in Chinese schools not only could not change the character of these people but also caused a great deal of opposition among them and strained relations with Nationalist China (Taiwan). But these critics seemed to forget that national sovereignty was important for its symbolic nature, and that most countries were sensitive over this symbolism.

National sovereignty figured prominently in Mr. Diem's dealings with the United States. Many Vietnamese understood his wariness in allowing U.S. advisors to be assigned to the district or battalion level for fear this would provide grist for the Communist propaganda mill.

In short, President Ngo Dinh Diem had proved to be a leader who showed much concern for his country and who had depth of vision and the ability to foresee political moves in his encounter with Communist North Vietnam. However, his mistake of overrelying on members of his family had led certain among them to excesses, especially Mme Nhu, who was so hated by the people that his own prestige was adversely affected. It must be conceded, however, that those on whom he relied the most such as Mr. Nhu and Mr. Can were truly competent; and given the precariousness of his position in 1954, it would not be hard to see that he probably could not have survived the two critical years after Geneva without his brothers. His next error was his unyielding attitude toward Buddhists which led to his final tragedy. People were usually forgetful but not about Mr. Diem. In the years 1971-73, when the situation became more difficult and society more divided, people remembered him, visited his grave, and held religious services in his memory on the anniversary of his death. This was probably the most eloquent commentary on his leadership. In these times when talking about Mr. Diem few referred to him as a dictator and many agreed that he and his actions were right.

After Mr. Diem's death, South Vietnam earned the reputation of having too many leaders who came and went too rapidly. This was a flaw in South Vietnamese politics, one that prompted pessimists to believe that Mr. Diem's death foreshadowed the demise of free Vietnam. In the Vietnam context, most people agreed that a political leader had to combine talent, integrity, and moral excellence with achievements and contributions to the country. Replacing or dismantling a regime was not difficult, but building a better government or finding a better national leader than Mr. Diem proved to be totally elusive to the efforts of both South Vietnam and the United States in later years.

Democracy and Leadership since November 1963

The overthrow of Mr. Diem and its causes served as a lesson for South Vietnamese leaders from November 1963 onwards, especially for governments that rapidly succeeded one another during the 1963-65 period. After the successful coup, General Duong Van Minh's government tried to win popular support with actions antipodal to those of Mr. Diem.

As a result Buddhism gained a strong position both as a major religion and a pressure group. In the RVNAF, this led to the creation of a Buddhist chaplain's organization similar to that of Roman Catholics. The United Buddhist Church received governmental support in expanding its organizations and building new places of worship, including a national pagoda.

The strategic hamlet policy, which had been accused of alienating the masses, was abolished by the junta's generals, particularly General Ton That Dinh, whose thoughtless comment on this matter had become a major cause for the collapse of the strategic hamlets although he later vehemently denied it. But General Minh's government floundered from the very beginning. While the people were expecting true reforms from the new regime, Mr. Minh retained Mr. Nguyen Ngoc Tho, who was Vice President under Mr. Diem, as the new Prime Minister. Mr. Tho was selected because he was a Southern-born Buddhist and an able administrator. Yet the people rejected him as being a holdover and regarded the new government as Diem's government without Diem.

The RVNAF ranks at that time seemed to consist of three groups: those who had joined the revolution, even at the last minute, and had been rewarded with fast promotions and appointments to key positions; those loyal to the old regime who had been jailed and relieved of their duties pending investigation; and those who belonged to neither side but were disillusioned with the first group.

In January 1964, General Nguyen Khanh's putsch brought down General Minh's government without a popular protest. Politicians loyal to the Diem regime placed high hopes on Mr. Khanh, once known as Mr. Diem's adopted son, to vindicate Mr. Diem's policies. But Khanh pursued his own ambition of becoming chief of state. Because his standing was so low, Khanh's politics were highly opportunistic in nature. Now he retained Mr. Minh as chief of state, now he replaced him by a troika (Minh, Khanh and Khiem). In August 1964 General Khanh proclaimed a new charter, known as the Vung Tau Charter, intended to replace the Constitution of the First Republic. According to this charter the chief of state would enjoy broad powers similar to those of France's General de Gaulle. As soon as the charter was announced, university students staged protest demonstrations fearing it would pave the way for military dictatorship. Though these demonstrations were mild and lacked the intensity of those pitted against Mr. Diem, they led to a rather strange conclusion. After a close encounter with demonstrating students Mr. Khanh personally tore the charter in pieces and, in unison with the students, he shouted, "Down with the Vung Tau Charter!" Though Mr. Khanh had been known as a brave airborne officer, he had to beat a hasty retreat when confronted with determined opposition because perhaps Mr. Diem's example was still fresh in everyone's mind.

Leadership in the South ran into total disarray from November 1963 to 19 June 1965, when the military finally took over. During that period there was no single leader with real power or a background worthy of being the captain of the ship of state. In a short period of eighteen months, therefore, South Vietnam had seen a succession of five cabinets led by Nguyen Ngoc Tho, Nguyen Khanh, Tran Van Huong, Nguyen Xuan Oanh and Phan Huy Quat. As a result, society went through a period of deep division and confidence crisis. Leading politicians opposed each other on the grounds of religion, which almost degenerated into an open religious conflict between Buddhists and Catholics.

It was also during this time that an attempt was made to return to civilian rule, but hitherto well-known civilian personalities proved to be inept politicians. Mr. Phan Khac Suu, a revolutionary who had been jailed in Con Son by the French and also jailed under Diem, accomplished nothing worthy of his position as chief of state. Instead he and his Prime Minister, Mr. Phan Huy Quat, squabbled so bitterly that power finally went back to the military in June 1965. The advantage of having a military government at this time lay in the fact that the people in general were fed up with political instabilities, and were expecting stronger leadership.

Once back in power, the military instituted a radical change in the designations of leadership positions. The position of chief of state was now Chairman of the National Leadership Committee, and was held by Lt. General Nguyen Van Thieu. The Prime Minister, Major General Nguyen Cao Ky, was called Chairman of the Central Executive Committee, and cabinet members were known as commissioners. This nominal change was intended to presage a new era of strong, revolutionary government.

Some of Mr. Ky's actions met with popular approval, such as the execution of Ta Vinh, a rich Chinese businessman in Cholon who had been found guilty of disrupting the nation's economy, and the assistance given to poor people. Mr. Ky also demonstrated he was a courageous man who would not hesitate to employ military force to put down protest demonstrations by extremist militant Buddhists in 1966, which were more massive than those confronting Mr. Diem in 1963 and even joined by almost all military units stationed in MR-1.

However, the fact that all political powers were concentrated in the hands of the generals became a matter of concern for many. To the Americans the military government was flawed by its not having been

popularly elected and the absence of a constitution. To political
factions, a government headed by the military was perhaps prelude to
dictatorship. These worries were not groundless because RVNAF generals
had become practically a new political force. National power was held
by the Armed Forces Council made up of ten generals among whom there
were the Chairman of the National Leadership Committee, the Chairman of
the Central Executive Committee, the Chief of the Joint General Staff,
and the Corps/MR commanders. It was the Armed Forces Council that voted
to let Thieu and Ky run for national office on condition that they carry
out the Council's decisions in accordance with the principle of collective
leadership and individual responsibility.

The Constitutional Assembly was elected on 15 January 1966 to draft
a Constitution for the Second Republic. During its sessions the consensus
among its 117 members was to build democracy in the South and to recognize
the right to political opposition. To reach this goal, the Assembly voted
Mr. Phan Khac Suu into the office of President of the Assembly.

When the new Constitution was unanimously approved on 18 March 1967,
the one thing that stood out clearly was that while the Constitution had
been intended to limit presidential powers by setting up a bicameral
national legislature and recognizing the right to form political parties,
it also conferred upon the President broad powers and advocated a two-
party system similar to that of the United States. Another important
point was that the Armed Forces Council now retained only an advisory
role to the President in matters of promotion and discipline.

The Presidential and Senate elections of September 1967 could be
considered honest and democratic. Six hundred foreign observers and
correspondents had been invited to witness these elections. Contrary
to Diem's election in 1960, servicemen received no orders to vote for
any tickets; they were completely free to vote for the candidates of
their choice. At the polls located in the Joint General Staff compound,
for example, a large number of the Thieu-Ky ballots were seen discarded
and scattered on the ground.

The 34% plurality with which Mr. Thieu and Mr. Ky won the election
faithfully reflected the constituents' impartiality and the degree of
democracy attained. Later on, however, critics both in the country and

in the United States seemed to dwell on this 34% plurality to prove how little popular support Thieu and Ky had won, but completely ignored the truly democratic nature of the election. For this reason one obsession of South Vietnamese governments in subsequent years was to achieve a high percentage at the polls at any cost. But such an excessive majority as 99.8% which was once reported only served to increase suspicion about the government's honesty.

The Second Republic lasted from 1 November 1967 until 30 April 1975. Mr. Thieu was the President almost throughout the period and resigned only one week before the collapse of the South. No matter what defense he could muster, he was responsible for this downfall. What then were Mr. Thieu's failures in leadership?

Mr. Thieu had leadership qualities. He was cautious, cunning, persevering, intelligent; he was also a courageous man. His visits to the battlegrounds of Kontum and An Loc in 1972 while the fighting was still raging prompted admiration for his courage, and his presence bolstered the morale of cadres and soldiers alike. Still there was a common belief that Mr. Thieu's ways to govern were those of an overlord incapable of winning hearts and minds. He was nominated by the Armed Forces Council to run for President after promising to abide by the principle of collective leadership. But once elected, Mr. Thieu acted counter to the council's wishes and was accused of foul play. He considered himself elected by the people, and having enjoyed U.S. support, he began to ignore and dismantle the very apparatus that had helped him to power. First, he moved to consolidate his position by eliminating other members of the Armed Forces Council such as Lt. General Le Nguyen Khang. General Khang was a close friend of Mr. Ky's, and both were graduated from the 1952 Class No. 1 of the Nam Dinh Reserve Officers' School. At the time General Khang was III Corps/MR-3 Commander, Commander of the Capital Military District and Saigon-Gia Dinh Military Governor, and commander of the Marine Division. The chief reason advanced by Mr. Thieu for replacing General Khang was that Khang was holding too many positions; the true but untold reason, however, was to reduce Vice President Nguyen Cao Ky's power. Lt. General Do Cao Tri, then Ambassador to South Korea, was recalled and given the post of III Corps/MR-3 Commander after the 1968 Tet Offensive, and Brigadier General Nguyen Van Minh was appointed Commander of the Military District Capital. General Khang thus found himself deprived of all positions except that of Marine Division Commander.

Another reason for General Do Cao Tri's assuming command of III Corps/MR-3, which did not become known until other members of the Armed Forces Council divulged it later, was that Mr. Thieu had wanted to replace General Cao Van Vien as Chief of the Joint General Staff. But since General Tri had been out of the country for a long time and needed to bring himself up to date on the organization and status of the RNVAF, his appointment as Chief, JGS had to wait. Meanwhile, once firmly in command of III Corps/MR-3, General Tri rallied behind Prime Minister Tran Van Huong and supported him. Suspicious of Tri's loyalty, Mr. Thieu abandoned the idea of replacing General Vien. On his part, when he learned about the President's intention to replace him, General Vien tendered his resignation but was repeatedly rejected. It was not that Mr. Thieu trusted General Vien as Chief of the Joint General Staff; in fact, he was using Vien. General Vien was a vegetarian on religious principles and certainly not power-hungry. Keeping him as Chief, JGS would free Mr. Thieu from worries about military coups and allow him to focus on other matters. Many believed that if the Chief, JGS, had been someone else, President Thieu would have had a harder time clinging to his presidency. Mr. Thieu's moves to replace key military personnel as well as his breach of trust against the Armed Forces Council adversely affected military solidarity, creating schisms that reduced the RVNAF performance. Ironically, the need to combat the Communists, who were the main enemies, seemed to get less attention from Mr. Thieu than political infighting and the consolidation of his power.

Being a soldier who had learned the trade of statecraft, Mr. Thieu regarded politics as a game of nerves and perseverance. A case in point was his repression of the veterans' struggle movement in Saigon. This movement broke out in April 1970 when disabled veterans decided that they had been neglected and abandoned by the government. Using the GVN land reform policy to guide their actions, they launched their slogan, "land to the farmers, home to the disabled veterans." Moving in groups, the veterans occupied public parks and vacant lots on both sides of city streets on which they erected shantytowns. When the police came they met with stiff resistance. The government moved gingerly and, taking that as a sign of victory, the disabled veterans engaged in further excesses that were finally condemned by everyone. Not until that time did Mr. Thieu order all veterans' leaders arrested. His cunningly timed action did not stir up a word of protest because it was clear to the public that the government was right.

Mr. Thieu began to come under heavy attack when he was preparing for his re-election to a second term in 1971. His opponents were Duong Van Minh and Nguyen Cao Ky. The election law had been revised with the objective of causing them the most difficulty. In May 1971 the Supreme Court accepted the candidacy of Mr. Minh and Mr. Thieu only; it rejected Mr. Ky's candidacy on technical grounds. Finally both Mr. Minh and Mr. Ky withdrew, apparently to undermine the election despite the fact that Mr. Ky's candidacy was later approved. This withdrawal left the field to Mr. Thieu's lone candidacy, a fact that gave rise to criticisms of a "one-man show" and dictatorship.

The Communists' 1972 General Offensive gave Mr. Thieu a chance to further strengthen his rule and weaken the opposition of political parties, the press, and other groups. He asked the legislative branch to grant him emergency powers to make laws for six months in order to handle the Communist general offensive. The Senate balked but the House gave him approval, and finally he got his way. With this power he declared a martial law in July 1972, which banned all strikes and acts, words, or pictures deemed detrimental to national security. The police were given the right to shoot to kill criminals in flight.

Next a press law was promulgated in August 1972 whereby, pending court proceedings, the government could suspend a newspaper that had been seized twice before for carrying articles harmful to national security and law and order. Each newspaper owner was also required to deposit a bond equivalent to US $47,000 to defray court costs and fines in case of litigation. The effect of this law was that 14 out of 41 Saigon newspapers had to close down for failure to meet new requirements; of the remaining ones, only two belonged to the opposition.

In September 1972 an executive order replaced the law for the election of village officials. This order empowered province chiefs to appoint village officials, saying explicitly, "In conclusion, although the administration process at the village and hamlet level has made some progress, it is no longer appropriate and capable of meeting the nation's requirements at the present stage of struggle against the Communists." This move was criticized as a regression from democracy. One day before Mr. Thieu's emergency powers were to expire, he promulgated a law governing political parties. According to this law, to qualify as such, each political party was required within three months to organize local chapters in at least one fourth of the hamlets in half of the nation's 44 provinces, and each local chapter's membership would have to number at least 5% of the local constituency. Each party had also to receive at least 20 percent of the votes cast in any national election, or it would have to be disbanded. This political parties' law met with strong criticism from opposition politicians who considered it even more restrictive than the previous law of 18 June 1968, and they all accused him of trying to eliminate all other parties except his Democratic Party, which alone could meet new requirements.

The Democratic Party was founded in November 1972 as a government's party similar to the Worker's Party in the North. Members were for the most part civil servants, administrative personnel, village officials, elected officials such as senators, representatives, city councilmen, province councilmen, all of whom were pro-government. Though a few generals also joined the Party, Mr. Thieu did not expand membership to the RVNAF and police, probably because he heeded the lesson of the Can Lao Party. A hasty organization riddled by careless membership screening, attention to numbers, and lack of a political platform, the Democratic Party was just a rallying point for those who sought personal benefits, a far cry from the Can Lao Party which it was intended to imitate.

The Paris Agreement of January 1973 forced Mr. Thieu to make preparations for a political struggle with the Communists. Therefore, he advanced a program of administrative revolution which purported to make cadres out of civil servants and send them to the countryside. Correct as its objective might appear, the program did not succeed inasmuch as civil servants, who had been accustomed to the easy life of urban areas, tried their best to avoid a rural assignment. On the other hand, putting urban civil servants in a rural setting would have been an unrealistic undertaking because of the incompatibility of life styles.

Popular discontent mounted after the complete withdrawal of U.S. forces. On top of military weaknesses there were economic disasters. The rank of the unemployed swelled to 800,000. Then came the devaluation of the piaster, runaway inflation, and the 1973 international oil crisis which further boosted prices. To fill the budget gap, income taxes were raised and new rates applied retroactively. This fiscal move gave rise to cries of crushing burden and injustice since the new tax burden lay heavily on small business while some 500 rich tax evaders remained immune from government action.

Mr. Thieu's move of changing the Constitution to allow him to run for a third term met with opposition in the Senate but was approved by the House; it was condemned as an act of sabotage against democracy and a prelude to dictatorship. Mr. Thieu was strongly attacked for following in Mr. Diem's footsteps, becoming more authoritarian and secluded with each passing day.

The U.S. Congress's move to cut aid to the RVN and President Nixon's difficulties in the Watergate affair were not lost on South Vietnamese opinion and began to destabilize Mr. Thieu's position. Mr. Thieu was now having to deal with his closest aides among whom was his political adviser, Nguyen Van Ngan, who was in charge of liaison with the National Assembly. This man bought senators' and representatives' allegiance with money to insure their support of Thieu's policies. Using the power given to him, Mr. Ngan sought in fact to consolidate his own position instead of Mr. Thieu's, going as far as seeking out lawmakers to cause Thieu trouble. So in May 1974 President Thieu fired Mr. Ngan. One month later 301 Catholic priests signed a proclamation against corruption, injustice, and social decadence. The proclamation quoted a statement of the Archbishop of Saigon in early 1974 which said, "This country could be lost because of corruption, especially corruption committed by persons in power."

The Roman Catholics had always been taking the government's side and enjoying the government's favors. Many maintained therefore that the Catholics, who anticipated a hard political struggle with the Communists in the days ahead, were taking the lead in cleaning up house and preparing the South for that contest.

The thrust of the anti-corruption movement led by Father Tran Huu Thanh was directed against Mr. Thieu's closest associates who had been long known for corruption such as the commanders of Military Regions 2, 3, and 4, the President's national security adviser, Lt. General Dang Van Quang, and Prime Minister Tran Thien Khiem. Mr. Thieu's inaction and President Nixon's resignation in August 1974 were partly instrumental in precipitating a change in the movement's targets. Mr. Thieu now personally came under direct attack. The movement made public its Indictment No. 1 in Hue on 8 September 1974 which cited six instances of corruption perpetrated by Mr. Thieu and members of his family. He was accused of having bought two villas in Vietnam at the cost of VN $138 million and one home in Switzerland and appropriated three hectares of choice land in the heart of Dalat City which cost VN $60 million, not counting land elsewhere. His brother-in-law was indicted for monopolizing the fertilizer industry, costing the people VN $30 billion. Mme Thieu sponsored the construction and operation of the Vi Dan (For the People) Hospital, which admitted only rich patients. Both Mr. Thieu and Prime Minister Khiem were charged in connection with a marijuana ring. Finally, a member of Thieu's family was accused of manipulating the rice market in MR-1 and making illegal profits. In support of these accusations, demonstrations succeeded one another to protest the government's corruption.

Mr. Thieu's ensuing cabinet reshuffle, his transfer of two MR commanders under accusation, and the discharge of a number of senior officers failed to satisfy the protesters. The reason was that a few cabinet members who lost their jobs had been known for their honesty such as the former Ministers of Finance and of Land Reform. The public therefore believed that Mr. Thieu's actions were motivated by other considerations than corruption charges because if these had been considered, Lt. General Quang should have been the first one to be fired. Also, a large number of field-grade officers who had been discharged were but disciplinary cases; others had been discharged for reasons other than corruption. The protesters therefore refused to be mollified and demanded President Thieu's resignation.

Although indications of a large-scale Communist offensive became apparent toward the end of 1974, the press and political personalities considered it a ploy when President Thieu called the nation's attention to this threat. This produced probably the most disastrous effect, one that led to the collapse of South Vietnam. Mr. Thieu had obviously lost the people's trust, and only the Communists stood to gain by it. For example, at the beginning of 1975 when the police discovered that several Vietnamese journalists were Communist and detained them, the entire press corps engaged in protests on the grounds of government frame-up and repression. There had always been a great deal of bad blood between President Thieu and the press corps which had criticized him on many counts. While these criticism seemed warranted by genuine opposition, there were also among Saigon newspapers several owned by pro-Communists.

Newspaper seizure under President Thieu's administration was a routine action. For example, 11 out of 41 Saigon papers were seized on 11 March 1972 for having published news considered detrimental to national security. In fact, the papers were merely protesting the government's decision to raise newsprint price by 125%; they attacked it as a move to choke off freedom of the press. Then, when it was made public, the Press Law of July 1972 ran into spirited opposition from the press corps. It forced many newspaper owners into financial difficulties, closed down many newspapers, and threw journalists out of employment. The press corps, therefore, resorted to all means to fight President Thieu and demolish his prestige. Indictment No. 1 of the anti-corruption movement, for instance, was carried in its entirety by three papers. In spite of their seizure, a large number of issues had reached the readership.

The press corps understandably showed a good deal of sympathy for the opposition, and eventually a collaboration among the press, the opposition, and the anti-corruption movement seemed to have emerged. On 30 September 1974, for example, 100 Catholic priests, Buddhist monks, and opposition leaders took to the streets in support of the fight for the freedom of the press. Gradually the opposition expanded its ranks by cooperating with other groups such as the Anti-Famine Movement and the Women's Movement for the Right to Life, both of which were clearly instigated by the Communists, but this fact seemed not to deter its actions against Mr. Thieu. In reality, though the police knew that Nun Huynh Lien and her anti-famine movement were part of a Communist front they did not dare to arrest her. Mme Ngo Ba Thanh, Chairperson of the Women's Movement for the Right to Life, was a Communist agent. Yet when she was arrested and sentenced to jail, so much protest arose from public opinion and even from the U.S. Embassy which regarded her primarily as an opposition leader that she was finally released.

South Vietnam in the final days prior to the collapse was like a patient going through a political delirium, unable to tell the truth from falsehood, and clamoring for Thieu's resignation without an idea of who would take his place or what would be the future course of the nation. The protesters opposed him on grounds of dictatorship and corruption, but none advanced any appropriate solution to the predicament of South Vietnam. Even if their demands had all been met, the fate of South Vietnam probably would not have fared better and perhaps would have been far worse than it was because of anarchy. Clearly, no one knew what balance to strike between total freedom and total restraint. This was a real crisis of democracy in the face of imminent threat to its survival.

All things considered, Mr. Thieu's regime was perhaps not as totalitarian as it appeared to be because what the opposition demanded might not even exist in a true democracy; besides, not everyone agreed that Mr. Thieu was a dictator. On the contrary, many were of the opinion that South Vietnam was a case of excessive democracy and freedom which bred a breakdown of law and order. Their main argument was that if South Vietnam was a dictatorship, then what would North Vietnam be called?

Generally speaking, the democratic experiment in South Vietnam was a failure of defining the limits of freedom and democracy for a country at war which had just recently been initiated to the democratic system of government. South Vietnamese leaders from 1954 to 1975 seemed to fall into two groups: weak demagogic leaders moved by opportunism and having no solid leadership qualities such as those emerging between 1963 and 1965 and strong leaders like Diem, Ky, and Thieu, who were opposed for being dictatorial. It must be conceded, however, that in spite of allegations to the contrary, South Vietnam did enjoy some measure of democracy which made possible at least two periods of stability. The trouble with South Vietnamese political parties, opposition leaders, and extremist young men was that they had gone too far in demanding unrestrained implementation of Western democratic practices. This self-delusion was aptly compared by Mr. Diem to "a child who wants to run before he can walk."

Some argued that leadership was the key to it all and that with good leadership South Vietnam would have been able to overcome its problems of political immaturity and lack of democratic experience. However, this ideal leadership was perhaps impossible to achieve. After a long period of French repressions followed by Communist treachery, South Vietnam no longer had any truly devoted and capable nationalist leader left who was worthier than Mr. Diem. His errors such as nepotism and favoritism for Catholics were not irremediable. In him people could at least discern the stature of a genuine leader and unequalled nationalist zeal. Mr. Thieu paled besides Mr. Diem in personal prestige. He did not have the necessary background for a leader of the people. He lacked what was termed as revolutionary virtue which the people in the South or North wanted to see in a national leader. The next flaw in his leadership was his overreliance on the United States, which kept him from planning ahead for the day when South Vietnam had to go it alone. Owing to U.S. policies he had been protected from coups d'etat. Yet his excessive trust in the U.S. President's authority had led him astray. He had probably deluded himself in thinking that what the President of the RVN could do, the U.S. President should be able to do also. He seemed to ignore the fact the U.S. Congress could also limit the powers of the U.S. President.

Finally, political infighting in South Vietnam, the internecine fight to the death among men in the same boat, could only benefit the Communists. Those South Vietnamese who had struggled for the implementation of democratic rights in times of war could not bring themselves to think that some of these rights did not even exist in a Western society in times of peace. Now that South Vietnam is suffering under the Communist yoke, these people have an eye-opening chance to see for themselves what democracy is or is not. Most probably they will not live long to see it.

CHAPTER VI

Observations and Conclusions

South Vietnamese society was clearly polarized into two segments, the rural and the urban, each with a way of life and attitudes entirely different from the other.

Rural society consisted of the majority of the population, the stolid people who toiled the year round amid verdurous rice fields and placid hamlets with patience and perseverance. This social group bore all the traditional aspects of the Vietnamese society for generations. Eighty years of French colonial rule and even the French-Viet Minh war brought little change to the environment and folk life of rural Vietnam. It was with the same social environment that South Vietnam greeted a new regime after the country's partition and the return of peace in 1954.

The average Vietnamese citizen living in the countryside was basically submissive to authority and leadership. For him the Confucian trinity "King-Teacher-Father" of traditional times represented perhaps what he revered most in his life. "The Emperor's law yields to village rules," a somewhat exaggerated dictum which depicted rural political life, did not imply anarchy. It simply reflected the large measure of autonomy and freedom enjoyed by rural folks under monarchial rule of former times. The Vietnamese people always equated "loyalty to the emperor" to patriotism, which was their own way of expressing love for their country despite deep attachment to their home villages. Without this patriotic spirit perhaps Vietnam would have long ceased to be a nation. That the Vietnamese nation had survived and continued to expand southward until it reached the confines of the Mekong Delta was certainly not a mere accident of history. But despite its homogenity and latent strength, rural society, the very force that had held the nation together, was in general non-combative and adverse to disturbances and changes. It readily accepted and submitted to the authority and guidance provided by the urban class.

Prior to the French occupation in the 19th century, the urban society of Vietnam was just a tiny minority. With the exception of Hanoi, the ancient capital, and Hue, the new seat of the Nguyen dynasty, very few Vietnamese towns qualified as cities in the modern sense. Most in fact did not look much different from the more prosperous villages. Saigon at the time was just a fishing village.

Under French rule cities proliferated and developed. A new class of urban people emerged. It consisted primarily of civil servants, private employees, businessmen and merchants, large landowners, servicemen, and workers. Their offspring attended newly created schools, learned and observed a lot more than rural children. Western ideas became widespread and gradually permeated the urban people's lives and modes of thinking. With this, the concepts of freedom and individualism began to take roots.

The influence of Western civilization on Vietnamese society had its good and bad side. The Vietnamese no doubt benefited from extended knowledge and initiation to science and modern technology. The cities, which quickly absorbed novel political philosophies, became the cradle of revolutionary movements fighting against French rule for national independence. All this meant progress and foreshadowed a bright outlook for Vietnam's future. Against this backdrop, however, a traditional culture was in the process of decaying. Old values rapidly vanished while a new order was yet to be established and the new excellence fully absorbed. Urban people only saw the decline of monarchy, which symbolized national sovereignty, and the subservience of their monarch to foreign authorities. The majority of men of letters formed by Western education turned their eyes toward the foreign world, worshipping individualism as a new creed and caring only for career advancement and personal wealth. The old scholar's pride, which had been symbolized by men such as Phan

Thanh Gian, Nguyen Tri Phuong, and Hoang Dieu no longer existed.[1] In time city dwellers were increasingly engrossed in the materialistic life of the petty bourgeoisie, constantly looking for more benefits and becoming self-seeking and wily in the process.

The onset of war against the French in 1946 saw most city dwellers seeking refuge in the countryside. Driven by patriotic ardor, many remained to continue the fight within the ranks of the Viet Minh. Others, deterred by hazards and hardships and often burdened by family responsibilities, chose to return to their urban habitat under the protection of the French Expeditionary Corps. The majority of Vietnamese city people consisted of these returnees, and most belonged to the petty bourgeois class. Selfish by nature, they were not prepared to make sacrifices for any cause. While most naturally preferred national independence, freedom, and private property and abhorred Communism in consequence, it was also true that they were little interested in the common good and most reluctant to struggle for it or for any other group.

Selfishness and factionalism, therefore, were the main traits of South Vietnamese urban society. Pushed to extremity by disruptive circumstances, these traits materialized into internecine infighting among religious sects and interest groups during the last few years of the French-Viet Minh war, for better exploitation of the people. All this occurred while the upper class jockeyed for positions under the indifferent eye of an ex-emperor chief of state whose role had been overcome by historical events.

Under these circumstances, the emergent political leadership of Ngo Dinh Diem, the partition of the country, and the massive exodus

---

[1] These were prominent scholars and mandarins of the Confucianist school who served the Nguyen dynasty with loyalty and a profound sense of duty. Unable to repulse the French invaders, they all committed suicide to keep national pride intact.

of North Vietnamese refugees came about as godsend events which revived national consciousness. The new government's efforts to piece together the fragments of South Vietnamese society and impart a wholesome vitality to it met with a most enthusiastic popular welcome. These were to solidify into a foundation for the regime of the First Republic.

Placing more emphasis on the requirement to mobilize national strength for a contest with Communist North Vietnam, President Ngo Dinh Diem instituted a limited democracy, reserving for himself vast and truly encompassing executive powers. The National Assembly, as a result, assumed the symbolic role of democracy's watchdog while the judiciary, in keeping with the national goals set forth by the executive branch, felt that it, too, had the obligation to serve the common effort. Despite its recondite philosophy, the regime's guiding doctrine, personalism, sought basically to elevate human dignity and develop democracy through hard work and combativeness. Therefore, the building of democracy was to be a step-by-step progress requiring time and patience.

To strengthen the regime, President Diem endeavored to develop the nation and enlist popular support. His effort to motivate the people took many forms and proved effective especially in the rural areas. This success was primarily due to his personal stature as a leader who inspired the people's respect. With the sophisticated urbanites, however, Mr. Diem was less successful. Despite his prestige and moral excellence, he seemed rather shy and reclusive. His manners and personality still reflected the antique formation of an old mandarin, which hardly aided him in the role of a people's seducer, especially among the urbanites of modern times. His methods of resolving problems related to national security and survival were regarded as those of a despot. Besides, some of his principal associates obviously committed grave errors.

The First Republic was criticized for three main flaws: family rule or nepotism, monolithic party rule, and discrimination on regional and religious grounds. From hindsight, it was quite understandable that during the incipient years of his rule President Diem had to rely on his brothers and other close relatives because of his loneness and unfamiliarity with South Vietnam's politics. In time, however, this gave rise to excesses by some of his family members, which became the source of popular discontent.

In a close and decisive contest with Communism which took place in the midst of divisive social forces, perhaps the formation of a vanguard, loyal political party to motivate and needle other organizations into constructive action would have been an acceptable necessity. But the predominance of a monolithic party entrusted with overriding powers in a regime purported to be democratic inevitably fueled discontent and led to discord and disaffection. Can Lao Party members as a matter of fact held almost all key positions in the administration and the military, and their ranks abounded with incompetents who had only an eye for favors and privileges. This system was particularly unfair to those truly capable elements who, because of pride or self-respect, refused to be subservient to the party or join it. Although suppressed, discontent was quite widespread.

Discrimination, whether on regional or religious grounds, was the main source of injustice in the use of manpower and personnel management. In religious matters, discrimination was further accentuated by the large favors granted to the Roman Catholic Church and total disregard for Buddhism. This embittered the Buddhists and added to their antipathy toward the regime. Eventually, Buddhist reactions reinforced by disaffected urbanites and the accomplices of some of Diem's most trusted henchmen brought about the downfall of the First Republic. With it were also gone the achievements accumulated by Mr. Diem during the nine years of his tenure.

As soon as the towering figure of the "dictator" ceased to dominate the South Vietnamese political scene, the cities seemed to live in an uproar of freedom, and South Vietnamese society became the stage for a rapid succession of kaleidoscopic tragi-comedy acts. The perceptive audiences discerned among these acts the progress of three major events. First, there was an experiment in boundless democracy in which religions and factions competed among themselves and with the military for power. Second, the involvement of the U.S. in South Vietnam was increasing; and third, the war was escalating without a definitive outcome in sight. All three events combined to bring about far-reaching consequences for the society of South Vietnam.

On the socio-political scene, the most dynamic force was perhaps the religions. The Roman Catholics and the Buddhists were the only organizations capable of rallying the popular masses. But both also seemed handicapped by their own excesses. The Roman Catholics under the First Republic drew fire upon themselves by exacting too much favor from a Catholic President. Their ostentatious display of organizational prowess under the leadership of Archbishop Ngo Dinh Thuc alienated the public and ruined the standing of the Catholic Church. However, after 1963, it was the Buddhists' turn to enjoy influence. Convinced that the new leaders owed them their ascendency to power, the Buddhists adopted a patronizing attitude toward the government, dictating their wishes and imposing their supremacy. The Buddhist Church's most glaring weaknesses were perhaps its involvement in politics and the rift between its two leadership factions. Buddhist excesses naturally met with reactions from Catholics, and most disturbances that occurred during the two-year period after 1963 could be attributed to this rivalry.

The leaders of the militant Buddhists were too politically ambitious to confine themselves to religious activities. With their followers, they took to the streets in 1966, which caught the government in a dilemma. If the government gave in to their demands, then the Catholics would follow suit, and this meant more trouble. But if the government chose to disperse the demonstrators by force, its action could be condemned as repressive. Relations between the government and religion became tense, disjointed. But it was finally the excesses of the extremist faction that shattered the Buddhist Church's influence while the moderates seemed to gain in credibility. The general consensus was that the militant monks, those who led the struggle movement, could hardly be termed truly devout because Buddhism is a religion, not a political doctrine. The essence of Buddhist philosophy is conversion, not conquest. Buddha taught us humility and to live in harmonious relations with others. He did not advocate retaliation or rivalry.

In contrast to the restlessness of religions, South Vietnamese political parties seemed to be too inactive. In the wake of the disastrous VNQDD armed revolt against French rule at Yen Bai in 1930, Vietnamese nationalist parties suffered heavy losses and appeared to be completely paralyzed. This decline was largely the result of harsh repressive measures by French authorities and the treacherousness of the Indochinese Communist Party.

Not until much later did nationalist parties seem to revive, but their feeble re-emergence was hampered by dependence on foreign assistance. Both the Phuc Quoc Hoi and the Dai Viet heavily relied on the Japanese to fight French colonial rule. The VNQDD and the Cach Mang Dong Minh Hoi could not raise any activities without the support of Chiang kai-Shek's Kuomintang. When these parties realized that they could not collaborate with the Communist Viet Minh, they all turned away from the resistance and cooperated with ex-emperor Bao Dai who had been allied with the French. After 1954, some of the old nationalist party leaders apparently looked forward to obtaining assistance from the U.S. But those few truly self-reliant parties that emerged subsequently seemed neither well developed nor adapted to a new environment.

Another characteristic of South Vietnamese nationalist parties was their divisiness and disarticulation. Unable to join forces for a much-needed alliance, they not only disagreed on ideologies but also opposed one another because of self-interests. It was perhaps this continuous strife for political hegemony and the race for lucrative spoils that gave rise to the unprecedented proliferation of political parties after 1963. The sad fact was that hardly any political party deserved to qualify as such. The leaders of the old generation had become senile, weary and could not catch up with new currents. Among the young, emergent leaders, very few had any stature or prestige. Above all the very ranks of these parties were split by contending new and old schools, and even those well-established parties of long standing were torn asunder by internal disputes. The purposes of most newly created organizations were dubious at best; there was never any question of their getting together, much less forming a cohesive political force.

Because of these shortcomings, no South Vietnamese political party had a significant popular following. With the exception perhaps of the VNQDD and Dai Viet, whose affiliation was quite extensive in the provinces of MR-1, no other parties were able to exert any local influence probably because they all seemed disorganized and ineffective. Some argued that the political involvement of major religions coupled with governmental obstructions was the cause for the failure of political parties to attract a popular following. There might be a grain of truth in that, but the overriding fact was that political parties in general had nothing to show for themselves that could attract followers. Besides, having gone through so many disillusions, the people also tended to be suspicious of parties and politicians as a whole. This popular apathy seemed to derive from the fact that political parties were mainly an urban product, and their leaders, who belonged to the urban petty bourgeois class, were never able to reconcile their egotistic interests with those of the peasants and the workers. As a general rule and by nature, most of them preferred to operate individually and separately, more for their self-interest than for a common cause. Their activities were therefore disjointed, opportunistic; they reflected neither a sincere desire to build political strength nor any well-defined, long range program of action. It was no small wonder that most political activists usually courted the government from which they expected favors. But if they were not satisfied, they would turn to opposition through demagoguery or with the backing of a religion. Over the years, therefore, political parties failed to produce any leader of promising stature. For South Vietnam, this was a most regrettable thing because political parties were supposed to be a proving ground for the nation's future leaders.

The phenomena of divisiveness, discrimination, and infighting were not only confined to religions and political parties; in fact, they existed in every stratum of South Vietnam's social fabric though in varying degrees. The problem of ethnic minorities, for one, was not as serious as foreign opinion had visualized and depicted. For one thing, the individual Montagnard tribes were far too small and too scattered; they spoke too many languages, and their culture was too

complex. Because of these differences, they were unable to form any
durable allegiance for any single purpose. The Montagnards therefore
seldom posed any problems for the GVN aside from those related to
benefits, treatment, and privileges. Had it not been for Communist
subversion, perhaps there would never have been any significant Montagnard issue. But the national conflict had turned the Montagnard
habitat into an arena of hot contest. The courtship of both Vietnamese
sides had the effect of polarizing the Montagnards into two camps just
as the ideological conflict had divided the Vietnamese in the lowlands.
Within this frame of mind, as long as the war continued, the prospects
of ethnic revolt remained a smoldering problem.

Infighting and divisiveness were nowhere as serious and damaging
as among the South Vietnamese themselves. Regional discrimination, for
one, was latent in every social group, every area of activity. At times
it broke out into open consciousness, but most of the time it was contained, repressed.

Factionalism, however, was an all-time scourge that affected the
entire fabric of South Vietnamese society. Under the First Republic,
factionalism was not too serious because after all there was just one
faction -- the Ngo clan -- that dominated all others. But after the
Ngo's, factionalism had become an epidemic that no medicine could ever
cure. There were so many clans, so many factions that any attempt at
bringing them together was just unthinkable. Since every faction was
contending for its own interests, it became wary of all others, and
each could only trust its own members. Every key office in the government, the military, the regligions, or civil organizations turned into
a small power nucleus around which revolved a clan, a faction.
Factionalism was also smoldering between the military and the civilians.
Civilian leaders tended to consider themselves more educated and held
the military in low regard. They did not want to associate with military leaders whom they derogatorily called "those martial elements."
On their part, the RVNAF leaders were proud of the powers they were
holding; they also disassociated themselves from civilian personalities
whom they considered effete, incompetent, and incomprehensible and
slighted as "tearoom politicians." The pairing of civilian and military

officials in the political arena of South Vietnam, therefore, appeared as odd as an uneven pair of chopsticks.

Social divisiveness reached its extreme perhaps under the acute form of infighting among individuals. The South Vietnamese urbanite of the post-colonial era proved to be too selfish. This came as a result of the perils and upheavals he had lived through since the Viet Minh took power. In the persons who held power and authority, selfishness became self-worship. Almost everyone deluded himself in thinking that he was superior to others and he alone deserved to be the leader of them all. This self-worship mentality was the source from which sprang up nearly two hundred political parties and associations and as many leaders during the few years that followed Mr. Diem's death. Thinking of only themselves as such, these leaders naturally opposed and attacked any rival who dared pose himself as an equal. In time, divisiness and infighting among individuals weakened every organization and defeated South Vietnam's every effort at rallying national strength for the common struggle. Even national leaders fought among themselves because of personal incompatibilities and differences or merely because of the unsociableness of their wives. It was a great tragedy that personal interests and pride could have taken precedence over the very survival of the nation.

For these reasons, South Vietnam's experiment in democracy unlimited during a period of a complex war, was a foregone failure. During the 20 months after the 1963 coup, as many as nine governments succeeded one another on the political scene. This was a vicious chain of events which saw a military government brought down by the military who installed a civilian government which in turn was torn apart by opposing civilian elements -- religion, political parties, students -- and had to turn over power of the state to the military. South Vietnam finally ended up with the generals back in power after two years of turmoil. The military had not loosened their grip on political power since then because despite elections designed to confer a constitutional base and a democratic form to the Thieu-Ky government, this government remained in essence a structure of military rule with a civilian outlook. This situation reflected the true balance of power prevailing in South Vietnam. The civilians, whose dynamic force derived from religions and political parties, were too divisive to win in any national election; they also proved ineffective in the exercise of power. There remained the military who, under these circumstances, constituted perhaps the only truly cohesive and well-organized force capable of contending successfully with the Communists. Civilian rule, for all its desirability, could not be enforced without endangering the nation's survival.

But why, as an antithesis to the Communists' party rule and totalitarianism, did a truly free democracy not work in South Vietnam?

Complete democracy is a complex form of government which is not only difficult to operate effectively but also requires knowledge, maturity, and goodwill on the part of the common people as well as politicians. In the first place the South Vietnamese, especially the urbanites, were by nature obstinate, self-centered people who did not readily tolerate a divergence of opinions, which was the essence of freedom. They seemed adverse to free discussions which contributed to new ideas and helped shape a constructive opposition. Consequently, any faction that ascended to power in South Vietnam invariably sought to dominate and crush its opponents, and those who enjoyed a majority never bothered to respect the minority. The contention between Catholics and Buddhists was a major case in point; neither group seemed to let the other alone once it had access to political power. Naturally, the group in disfavor fought back for its own life, and the struggle for survival never seemed to come to an end.

The tendency of self-worship or self-supremacy on the part of political and religious leaders also allowed no chance for prospects of compromise. They seemed unwilling to admit that the rules of the game called for a broad spectrum of participation, that every participant was entitled to have its own voice, and that opinions sometimes differed or even opposed one another. Hardly any leader recognized the simple fact that no one could possibly hold all the truth and all the knowledge and that the essence of harmonious cooperation lay in tolerance and compromise. Unfortunately, it was a fact of South Vietnamese political life that almost every leader regarded himself as "the one and only." This was also true of religious leaders who engaged in politics but could not see beyond the confines of their church or of suspicious military leaders who did not want any civilian participation in state affairs. In retrospect, South Vietnam during the war was not a good soil in which the seeds of a true democracy could germinate.

Another obstruction to the democratic process was antagonism between freedom and order. The South Vietnamese urbanite cherished freedom and loathed everything that interfered with his private life or business. Naturally, as any free and selfish individual, he tended to maximize his freedom. But this yearning for maximum freedom conflicted with order and control that society required to avoid chaos. Our ever-present Communist enemy also took advantage of excessive freedom to intensify his subversive activities. His agit-prop agents, therefore, always joined in every clamor for more democratic freedoms. Obviously as long as South Vietnam struggled with this enemy for its own life, it still found it hard to reconcile what benefited the individual with the common good of society.

To the rulers of South Vietnam, complete democracy was apparently too sluggish and inefficient to fight the war. It neither guaranteed policy continuity nor adapted well to an emergent nation struggling for its own survival. Indeed, the co-option of policies through open debates and the quest for consensus among political groups and within the national assembly were not processes that could be achieved rapidly. A country at war perhaps needed some other modality by which it could make timely decisions; to achieve this, a concentration of authority seemed to be indicated. Democratic processes such as opinion polls, hearings, and debates, were procedures better suited for nations living in peace. Above all, the requirements of the fight against Communism clearly dictated a continuity in national policies. Undoubtedly, this concern for policy continuity was the major motive that had prompted military leaders to take over power especially when the situation was getting out of control.

Democracy, though desirable, is a complex way to govern a country. For South Vietnam, this process of government proved even more complex. Building democracy was not just a matter of producing a constitution adapted from Western countries or duplicating many of their formal institutions. The dangers lay in the insistence upon these formalities because they conveyed the impression that every freedom was permissible in the name of democracy. But even the founding fathers of the French and U.S. constitutions had found it necessary to institute a democracy with certain limits because it was a slow process of development. Like a tree, democracy could only develop if it had time to germinate, take roots, and grow. In South Vietnam, the urban society and especially politicians did have a sincere desire for democracy, but they lacked the patience and goodwill to allow their democratic infant to grow and mature. Besides, the true process could only start from the grassroots level, never from the top. During all this time the rural society, which was the starting point for this democratization process, never had the chance to live in security. Given a time for peaceful settlement, the villages of South Vietnam, with their prevailing sense of discipline and order, and which had for generations lived democratically by tradition and in spirit, would have been the very proving ground for a stable and durable democracy.

The early imposition of a Western-style democracy on South Vietnam, therefore, resulted in many problems. The infighting among factions was so vicious that a civilian prime minister became disenchanted with politics and relinquished his government to the military who put up a democratic front by producing a constitution and holding elections. No doubt, this was dictated by circumstantial needs because the U.S. insisted on some form of democracy to facilitate its provision of aid. But the democratic make-up failed to make the regime a democracy in its true sense. It was the kind of democracy in which elective offices were all held by military appointees and the executive ruled with emergency legislative powers by restricting both opposition and certain vital freedoms. It was a half-hearted democracy whose true nature was autocracy. But under pressure from U.S. public opinion which had a basic penchant for democracy, this turned out to be a weak and trembling autocracy. Suspicious and wary of opposition, this autocracy did not even dare crack down on opposing elements such as the anti-war An Quang faction. Although demonstrations were strictly forbidden, they still occurred, and the police were under orders not to interfere. Many of these unusual social and political manifestations reflected the controversial influence exerted by the United States.

The U.S. was unquestionably the mentor who raised the South Vietnamese infant and trained him into a strong adult. That South Vietnam existed at all as a nation and for that long was chiefly due to U.S. support. The fact was that by signing the 1954 Geneva Agreements, France already wrote off South Vietnam, convinced that it would inevitably come under Communist rule after the 1956 elections. U.S. support for President Diem had brought the situation around and played an important part in building South Vietnam into a separate, viable nation. However, the involvement of Americans, who represented a dynamic civilization, in a nation whose culture was essentially static seemed not very successful in producing a completely satisfactory relationship. The cultural differences between Americans and Vietnamese are antipodal. Americans are active, impatient, and rationalistic contrasted to Vietnamese who are quiescent, patient, and sentimental. Joining forces for a common effort, Americans and Vietnamese often saw the same problem differently, had different basic concepts, and acted and reacted in different ways. Under the First Republic American influence was not pervasive because the regime's leaders were self-assured and strong-minded to the point of becoming obstinate. U.S. assistance then was substantial but restrained. Discordance finally contributed to the downfall of a regime regarded by Americans as irredeemable. After that U.S. involvement in South Vietnam's own affairs seemed to have no bounds.

Militarily the U.S. had saved South Vietnam from dangers of collapse in 1965 by deploying its combat troops and fighting the ground war. The RVNAF were gradually expanded, modernized, and trained for combat under American military doctrine. Evidently, maintaining such a large and modern military force and ensuring its continued capability for combat demanded big expenditures that only a long-range aid program could provide. This was a most critical problem because South Vietnam's performance in self-defense depended primarily on that aid.

The protracted war, meanwhile, had ravaged South Vietnam's national resources and made a shambles of its economy. To help South Vietnam make ends meet, the U.S. poured in financial and material aid. But this aid seemed to benefit the urban sector mostly because the cities prospered as a result of war-related businesses and lucrative services rendered to U.S. and FWMAF troops while the rural people continued to labor in hardships amidst the hazards of an escalating war. Those familiar with the war scene of the 1965-1969 period certainly witnessed the overabundance of luxurious goods in the streetstands of big cities and the thriving black market and war profiteering. This only spoiled the urban society, widened the war wounds, and deepened social injustices. The GVN policy of overflowing the domestic market with imported goods because of budgetary needs did not help build an economy geared for long-range development. So when the U.S. began to reduce its involvement, South Vietnam's economic and social difficulties remained very much the same if not more serious.

The ubiquitous presence of Americans in almost every area of South Vietnamese government reflected a conspicuous truth: American initiative in the war. Through its hard-working, devoted, and efficient military and civilian advisers who commanded sizable means and resources, there was no doubt that the U.S. wanted to do it quickly and get it over with in the shortest time possible. This desire for quick results committed the U.S. to bigger expenditures which proved costly in the long run. American initiative also stifled South Vietnam's self-reliant spirit and made South Vietnamese, especially the urbanites who were dependent by nature, increasingly passive. For a developing nation facing the dangers of Communist subversion, this was a serious flaw that might prove fatal someday. The American experience seems to indicate that small nations fighting against Communism with U.S. aid would have been better off if they had endeavored to do things by themselves. Self-reliance should be a motto worth promoting.

American initiative and the deep American involvement in every aspect of South Vietnam's national endeavor brought to light another ill effect on the South Vietnamese national cause. The towering and conspicuous role of the U.S. as a "big brother" gave the impression that everything had been preordained by the U.S. The end result perhaps was that, in the eyes of world and domestic opinion, no GVN after 1963 ever enjoyed any measure of prestige because nobody believed that it was truly independent. Internally and internationally, this was damaging for South Vietnam's national cause because the war was essentially a political conflict. The enemy was thus given more grist for his propaganda mill, and much of the world at large also doubted the validity of South Vietnam's cause and its ability to fight. What should have been clearly defined and emphasized in a conflict like the Vietnam war was perhaps the exact relationship between the country that gave aid and the one that received it, the exact role to be played by each, and the rules that governed the common effort so as to enhance fully, not to stifle, the indigenous cause.

South Vietnam's over-reliance and total dependence on the U.S. strongly suggested a big void in national leadership, which was perhaps one of its gravest basic shortcomings. The apparent lack of vision, prestige, and strong-mindedness on the part of South Vietnamese leaders accounted for the nation's failure to enhance its cause through self-reliance. The First Republic's leadership had undoubtedly earned its prestigious reputation because of its hard-line approach to national affairs and articulate and cohesive policies. Although this prestige and strong-mindedness sometimes verged on vanity and intransigence, which did not please the U.S., in the eyes of a large segment of South Vietnamese those were the very traits of a strong and capable leadership. By comparison, the Second Republic's leadership seemed irresolute and unsure of itself. Its major flaw was too much preoccupation with power infighting and a rather opportunistic approach to solving national problems.

If Mr. Diem's regime had often been described as despotic and politically monolithic, his rule had also, in a certain sense, a salutory effect on South Vietnamese society. Because of this single-party system, national authority was strong and encompassing; everyone was required to submit to this authority, and order was enforced. For the nation-building effort of a developing country, this must have been beneficial. But after dismantling autocratic rule, South Vietnam found itself splintered into tiny power groups and too many political parties, all vying for political supremacy and suspecting and hurting one another in the process.

Added to this chaotic power struggle, there were also deep-seated discords and infightings between individuals, between religions, and between the civilians and the military. Because of this tumultuous internal strife national authority was shattered, order could not be maintained, and there was no longer any sense of national unity. Continuous disorder and changes taught the South Vietnamese to be wiser and more cautious, because your subordinate of today might well be your superior of tomorrow. Without being told, therefore, everyone became wary and adopted a wait-and-see attitude. In the public service, no one seemed completely eager to enforce control or to demand productivity; in fact, no one seemed fully dedicated for the public good.

Under the First Republic, there was only one Mme Nhu, but after her, there seemed to be too many Mme Nhu's in miniature. The fact was that in the inner circle of every power faction, there was always a Mme Nhu. In contrast to the Mme Nhu of the First Republic who promoted women's rights, organized women's movements, and heavily engaged in politics, her successors participated in businesses, bought and sold influence, sponsored new clans, and disliked each other. This caused rumblings among the public and dispirited the honest public servant.

Mr. Diem had been criticized for discrimination and cronyism in the appointment and promotion of personnel, but somehow his favoritism was limited, and the number of people who benefited from it did not seem too large. Despite criticisms, his methods of personnel selection were rigorous, and the standards of qualification restrictive but meritorious. After 1963, however, cronyism and favoritism seemed to have no limits. Each center of power, each faction nominated its own henchmen to key positions. Fairness and the criteria of talent and morality no longer mattered. The public, therefore, witnessed personnel promotions and transfers "en masse" without any justification which, in the years ahead, was to bring about enormous difficulties in personnel management.

The fact that the majority of middle and low-echelon cadres issued from the urban petty bourgeois class did not help improve national leadership because of their intrinsic shortcomings. The young urban people in general loved freedom and welcomed any change for a better society, but they were also unrealistic and impatient. To motivate them and enlist their enthusiastic participation in the common effort, constant coaxing and incentives were required. But the leaders of the post-Diem era seemed to have missed every good opportunity to put the urban youth's patriotic ardor and anti-Communist dedication to work. These opportunities existed immediately following the overthrow of Mr. Diem in 1963 when the cities were alive with revolutionary passion, then at the height of the Communist offensive in 1968 when almost every urban youth felt it a duty to join the military service, and finally after South Vietnam was given a chance to stand on its own during the redeployment of U.S. forces. That included the sobering jolt brought about by the 1973 Paris Agreement. This failure to foster the urban revolutionary zeal and use it for the anti-Communist fight seemed to stem from our leaders' very lack of foresight and dependence on the United States.

It came as no surprise, both in the eyes of the public and in the belief in knowledgeable quarters, that every national endeavor and the conduct of the war itself totally conformed to American policies. In time the very survival of South Vietnam came to depend on the will and support of the U.S. Having nothing left to decide and to show for its valor, the South Vietnamese leadership gradually lost all prestige and real authority. This void in leadership loomed larger than ever after the U.S. withdrew all of its troops, settled for a peace arrangement, and reduced its involvement. The ranks of South Vietnamese leadership, who heretofore had proved readily amenable to U.S. wishes, now found themselves hopelessly vulnerable, unable to stand on their own feet, and utterly incapable of pulling the nation together.

After their fortunes had gone through so many ups and downs, the South Vietnamese people became wiser but they did not seem to believe whole heartedly in the future of South Vietnam. This explained why South Vietnamese society became dispirited and devoid of the will to continue struggling. It was not surprising that the wealthy and the influential transferred funds to foreign accounts and sent their children abroad. This was also true of some of our national leaders who found it more reassuring to provide for their own uncertain future. And those who could not do otherwise just let themselves flow along, living a life without tomorrow. This hopeless situation manifested through the proliferation of anti-war literature, arts, and music and the increasing numbers of youths and misfits indulging themselves in debauchery. It also accounted for widespread draft dodging and the lowering morale among the ranks of civil servants and servicemen. All this seemed to explain why a military force of over one million men plus a significant police force and some four million PSDF members were incapable of maintaining territorial security throughout South Vietnam.

The picture thus depicted of South Vietnamse society was indeed bleak and dark, but it did not imply that all South Vietnamese had lost the will to survive and continue the fight. Certainly not all servicemen, civil servants, and policemen neglected their duties or shunned their responsibilities. There were in fact many segments of the South Vietnamese population which still proved aggressively anti-Communist, and the majority of RVNAF servicemen, national policemen and civil servants continued to fight and serve with dedication and purpose in the hopes that somehow the situation was going to improve. Indeed, there had been too many shiny examples of heroic sacrifices among their ranks to attempt to prove the contrary. In general, no matter what had happened, the South Vietnamese people had displayed throughout the war a most laudable spirit of endurance and resiliency that few other peoples could match.

On the other hand, a comparative study of developing nations under similar conditions revealed that our leadership was after all not as bad as it might appear. Perhaps our leaders still had to prove they could measure up to their tasks and responsibilities in meeting the challenge of combat and conducting the complex war efforts effectively. In the South Vietnamese context, perhaps they still had to prove that they stood by and fully matched the immense sacrifices and sufferings of our people.

Despite its complexity, the problem of South Vietnamese society revealed certain well-defined basic requirements that were to be met satisfactorily in order to motivate, rally, and unite this inherently anti-Communist popular mass. The first requirment was capable leadership. The national leader should have been someone who had prestige, moral excellence, and talent to inspire respect, trust, and obedience. Then he should have been clear-sighted enough to surround himself with a competent and dedicated staff and create a governmental apparatus completely responsive and devoted to public service. Such a leader would surely inspire the cadres and public servants to perform better. Under this leadership, the armed forces would also fight with more dedication and behave correctly toward the people.

The second requirement was to ensure security and protection for the rural people. To achieve this, South Vietnam would have required an all-efficient and thoroughly polyvalent military force and a professional police force which enjoyed a good rapport with the people. Popular confidence and trust in these forces would help overcome their shortcomings and enhance the solidarity and combined strength between them and the people. Security would make it possible to build and develop the nation and the rural people would certainly benefit from it materially because South Vietnam was not without national resources.

The third and last requirement was to assuage the ardent desire for democracy and freedom on the part of the urban people. But to achieve this without giving a free hand to subversive and pro-Communist elements would certainly require a gradual process of breaking-in. We believe that as long as the subversive war continued, there could not be any question of complete democracy and unlimited freedom. What the government could have done, however, was to accept genuine opposition and allowed it a decent posture as well as certain well-defined freedoms in the nation's political life. Then, as control was assured and the war wound down as it had for sometime after the cease-fire, the government could have permitted less and less restraints until there were no more grounds for continued clamoring. For this course to achieve success, the leadership should abide by the rule of laws and above all set the example of courage, dedication, integrity, and moral excellence. The problem of South Vietnam, after all, was perhaps not democracy versus dictatorship but essentially a matter of how much democratic freedom we could afford at a certain given time.

Unfortunately, the problem of South Vietnam had not been thoroughly understood and correctly solved. Hampered by shortsightedness and retrogression, the class of leaders had lost its ability to lead. Society was torn asunder by internal strife, and the popular mass no longer had faith in the government. It semeed as if the vicious and drawn-out war had drained South Vietnam of all its vital resources and brought it to the brink of moral and material bankruptcy. So when the U.S. Congress decided it no longer desired to support a continuing war, most people could readily sense that the fate had been sealed for South Vietnam.

Glossary

CIDG	Civilian Irregular Defense Group
DAO	Defense Attache Office (U.S.)
FULRO	Front Unifié pour la Lutte des Races Opprimées (Unified Front for the Struggle of Oppressed Races)
GVN	Government of (South) Vietnam
ICP	Indochinese Communist Party
JGS	Joint General Staff
MACV	Military Assistance Command, Vietnam (U.S.)
MEDCAP	Medical Civic Action Program (U.S.-initiated)
MR	Military Region
NLF	National Liberation Front (of South Vietnam)
PSDF	People's Self-Defense Forces
RF/PF	Regional and Popular Forces
RVN	Republic of Vietnam
RVNAF	Republic of Vietnam Armed Forces
SEATO	Southeast Asia Treaty Organization
USAID	United States Agency for International Development
VCI	Viet Cong Infrastructure
VNQDD	Viet Nam Quoc Dan Dang (Vietnam Nationalist Party or Kuomintang)